THE PERENNIAL SCOPE
OF PHILOSOPHY

THE
PERENNIAL SCOPE
OF PHILOSOPHY

by

KARL JASPERS

Translated by Ralph Manheim

ROUTLEDGE & KEGAN PAUL LTD
LONDON

*First published in England 1950
by Routledge & Kegan Paul Limited
68–74 Carter Lane London E.C.4
Printed in Great Britain
by Latimer Trend & Co Plymouth*

CONTENTS

Chapter One

WHAT IS PHILOSOPHICAL FAITH?

IF WE ASK: by what and toward what shall we live, one answer will no doubt be: by revealed faith; for outside it there can be only nihilism. A theologian recently declared: 'It is no mere presumption on the part of the Church to say that the crucial alternative is: Christ or nihilism.'—If this were the case, there would be no philosophy. There would be on the one hand a history of philosophy, that is, a history of unbelief leading to nihilism, and on the other hand a system of concepts in the service of theology. Philosophy itself would be deprived of its heart, and where a theological atmosphere has prevailed, this has indeed been its lot. Even when works of consummate intellectual artistry have been created in such an atmosphere, they have taken their mood from an alien, non-philosophical source, ecclesiastical religion; their independence has been borrowed and illusory, and they have not been taken quite seriously as philosophy.

Another answer to our question is that we should live by human reason, by the sciences, which point to meaningful aims in the world and teach us methods of achieving them. For apart from the sciences, it is said, there are only illusions. Philosophy is not autonomous; step by step it has sloughed off all the sciences, and in the end even logic has become a specialized science. So that by now nothing is left.—If this were so, there would again be no philosophy. Philosophy was once a road to the sciences. Now at best it can drag on a more or less superfluous existence as a handmaiden to the sciences, perhaps in the form of epistemology.

But both these conceptions seem to contradict the inner meaning of philosophy in the three millennia of its history in China, India and the West. They are incompatible with the seriousness of our attitude toward philosophical problems to-day, at a time when philosophy has ceased to be the handmaiden of the sciences as it was towards the end of the nineteenth century, yet has not relapsed into a position of subservience to theology.

These facile alternatives of revealed faith or nihilism, of total science or illusion, serve as weapons of spiritual intimidation; they rob people of their God-given responsibility and make them subservient. They rend human possibilities into antinomies, and authentic humanity is forgotten.

Those who accept such alternatives declare that any one who dares to carry on the venerable tradition of philosophy must either be a nihilist or an illusionist. And if we do not live up to the preconceived picture, we are reproached with shallowness, inconsistency, trivial rationalism, unworldliness; we are attacked from both sides, by the proponents of an exclusive revealed faith and of a 'science' that has developed into super-stition.

We shall take up this challenge. We shall attempt to keep open the horizons of humanity in our philoso-phical thinking. Philosophy must not abdicate. Least of all to-day.

We live in the awareness of perils that were unknown to past centuries; our communication with the men of other ages may be broken off; we may heedlessly deprive ourselves of tradition; human consciousness may de-cline; there may be an end to open communication among men. In view of the dangers with which we are faced, we must in our philosophizing prepare for every eventuality, in order that our thinking may help humanity to preserve its highest potentialities. Pre-cisely because of the catastrophe that has overtaken the Western world, philosophical thought can regain full independence only by discovering its relation to the primal source of humanity.

I wish to speak to you of philosophical faith, which underlies all these ideas. The subject is vast. In order to stress certain simple principles, I shall divide our in-quiry into six lectures:

1. What is philosophical faith? 2. Contents of philo-sophical faith. 3. Man. 4. Philosophy and religion. 5. Philosophy and antiphilosophy (demonology, deifi-cation of man, nihilism). 6. The philosophy of the future.

Faith is a different thing from knowledge. Giordano

Bruno believed and Galileo knew. Outwardly they were both in the same situation. An inquisitorial court demanded of them both a retraction on threat of death. Bruno was willing to retract certain of his propositions, but not those which he regarded as essential; he died a martyr's death. Galileo retracted his theory that the earth revolved around the sun, and according to the apt but apocryphal anecdote later remarked: *Eppur si muove*. Here is the difference: On the one hand we have a truth that suffers by retraction, and on the other a truth which retraction leaves intact. Both men acted in keeping with the truth they stood for. A truth by which I live stands only if I become identical with it; it is historical in form; as an objective statement it is not universally valid, but it is absolute. A truth which I can prove, stands without me; it is universally valid, unhistorical, timeless, but not absolute; rather it depends on finite premises and methods of attaining knowledge of the finite. It would be unfitting to die for a truth that is susceptible to proof. But at what point the thinker who believes he has plumbed the depths, cannot retract his statements without harm to the truth itself—that is his own secret. There is no universal principle demanding that he become a martyr. But when, like Bruno, he suffers martyrdom, not out of emotional enthusiasm, not out of the defiance of the moment, but after a long and arduous conquest of himself, he reveals authentic faith, that is, certainty regarding a truth which I cannot prove as I can prove a scientific theorem regarding finite things.

WHAT IS PHILOSOPHICAL FAITH?

Nevertheless the case of Bruno is unusual. For philosophy is not ordinarily concentrated in propositions that assume the character of a credo, but in intellectual statements that bear upon existence as a whole. That Socrates, Boethius, Bruno are in a sense the saints of philosophy, does not make them the greatest philosophers. But they are revered for vindicating a philosophical faith after the manner of martyrs.

As against the platitude that man might base everything on his intelligence—if only there were no stupidity or ill will, everything would be all right—as against this rationalistic delusion, but still on the terrain of the rational, we designate the other thing to which we are bound as the irrational. One may reluctantly accept this irrational element, or one may cultivate it as an intrinsically unimportant play of the emotions, as an illusion indispensable to the psychic organism, as recreation for one's leisure time. One may even find in this irrational element forces to which one appeals as psychological passions, in order to achieve certain aims with their help. Or, finally, one may find the truth in these forces and plunge into the irrational, taking frenzy for authentic life.

But faith must not be taken to mean the irrational. This polarity of rational and irrational has only led to confusion. The insistence, now on science, now on some undiscussible and supposedly ultimate instance, the tendency to invoke now reason, now emotion, has given rise to an endless exchange of opinions without communication. Such a game was possible as long as the light of a great tradition, though growing steadily weaker, still served as a beacon. The life of the spirit ended when man knowingly based it on the irrational. It burned itself out in cheap attacks on everything, in stubborn adherence to arbitrarily selected ideas which were held to be effective, in the frivolous squandering of tradition through a seemingly superior freedom, and in high-sounding unreliable statements. All this cannot be combated, for there is no adversary to grapple with, but only an opaque, shifting, Protean muddle, so ephemeral that the intellect cannot pin it down; this situation can be surmounted only by determination to think clearly.

The irrational is at bottom mere negation; our faith cannot be a plunge into the darkness of anti-reason and chaos.

Philosophical faith, the faith of the thinking man, has always this distinguishing feature: it is allied with knowledge. It wants to know what is knowable, and to be conscious of its own premises.

Unlimited *cognition*, science, is the basic element of philosophy. There must be nothing that is not questioned, no secret that is withheld from inquiry, nothing that is permitted to veil itself. It is through critique that the purity and meaning of knowledge are acquired, and the realization of its limits. Anyone who engages in philosophical activity can protect himself against the encroachments of a sham knowledge, against the aberrations of the sciences.

Philosophical faith must also *elucidate* itself. When I

philosophize, I accept nothing as it comes to me, without seeking to penetrate it. Faith cannot, to be sure, become universally valid knowledge, but it should become clearly present to me by self-conviction. It should become unceasingly clearer and more conscious, and by becoming conscious unfold more and more of its inner meaning.

What then is faith?

In it, the faith through which I am convinced, and the content of faith, which I comprehend—the act of faith, and the faith that I acquire by this act—*fides qua creditur* and *fides quae creditur*—are inseparable. The subjective and the objective side of faith are a whole. If I take only the subjective side, there remains a faith that is merely a believing state of mind, a faith without object, which in a manner of speaking believes only itself, a faith without inner content. If I take only the objective side, there remains a content of faith, as object, as proposition, as dogma, as inventory, as a dead something.

Thus faith is always faith in something. But neither can I say that it is an objective truth that is not determined by faith but determines it—nor can I say that it is a subjective truth that is not determined by the object but determines it. Faith is one in that which we separate as subject and object, as faith by which and in which we believe.

Accordingly, when we speak of faith, we shall have in mind this faith that comprehends subject and object. Therein lies the whole difficulty of defining faith.

Here we must recall the great doctrine of Kant, which has its precursors in the history of both Western and Asiatic philosophy, whose basic idea inevitably made its appearance wherever men philosophized, but which only with Kant—here too in historical form but in its essential outlines valid for all time—was worked out consciously and methodically and became an element of philosophical elucidation. It is the idea of the phenomenality of our existence in its division into subject and object, bound to space and time as forms of sensibility, to categories as forms of thought. All being must be objectified for us in such forms, it becomes phenomenon for us, it is for us as we know it, and not as it is in itself. Being is neither the object that confronts us, whether we perceive it or think it, nor is it the subject.

The same is true of faith. If faith is neither solely content nor solely an act of the subject, but is rooted in the vehicle phenomenality, then it should be conceived only in conjunction with that which is neither subject nor object but both in one, with that which manifests itself in the duality of subject and object.

We call the being that is neither only subject nor only object, that is rather on both sides of the subject-object split, *das Umgreifende*, the Comprehensive. Although it cannot be an adequate object, it is of this, and with this in mind, that we speak when we philosophize.

Faith, it would appear, is *immediate*, in contrast to everything that is mediated by the understanding. Faith would then be an experience, an experience of the

Comprehensive, that either falls to my lot or does not fall to my lot.

But in such a conception, the ground and primal source of our being seems to slip into the psychologically describable, into contingency. Hence Kierkegaard says: 'What Schleiermacher calls religion, and the Hegelian dogmatists faith, is at bottom nothing other than the first immediate condition for everything—the vital fluidum—the spiritual atmosphere that we breathe.' (Journals, I, 54.) Anything 'that is so volatilized, so dissolved in mist' (Kierkegaard is here referring to Christianity) is not faith.

For Kierkegaard an essential attribute of faith is that it relates to a unique historical event and is itself historical. It is not experience, not something immediate that can be described as given. It is rather a primal awareness of being through the mediation of history and thought.

Philosophical faith realizes this. It looks on all formulated and written philosophy only as preparation or recollection, only as inspiration or confirmation. Hence no meaningful philosophy can be a self-contained conceptual system. The conceptual structure is never more than half, and attains to truth only if, in addition to being conceived, it is embodied in the thinker's own historical existence.

Hence the philosopher freely confronts his own thoughts. Philosophical faith must be characterized negatively: it cannot become a credo. Its thought does not become dogma. Philosophical faith is not firmly grounded in anything objective and finite in the world, because it merely uses its propositions, concepts and methods, and does not subordinate itself to them. Its substance is purely historical and cannot be anchored in the universal—though it is only in the universal that it can express itself.

Accordingly philosophical faith must continually draw upon the primal source within each historical situation. It achieves no rest in a body of doctrine. It remains a venture of radical openness. It cannot invoke itself as ultimate authority, but must manifest itself by thought and reasoning. Even the pathos of the inevitable statement that sounds like revelation constitutes a danger to philosophy.

The universality of true faith cannot however be formulated as a universally valid statement, it cannot be accepted as immediate, or objectively fixed as a product of history; we can only ascertain it historically by following the movement of time. But this occurs in the *realm of the Comprehensive*, which is neither exclusively subject nor exclusively object. The presence that always manifests itself historically includes within itself the sources of all faith.

In order to understand what faith is, we would have to elucidate the Comprehensive. The always mediated, for ever new immediacy of the Comprehensive, that which is always present, has several modes. In our description, the Comprehensive appears in a multiplicity of its modes. I shall here avail myself of a schema resulting from our philosophical tradition. In this place

I can set it down briefly (and I must ask you for a few moments to attempt the impossible with me, to attempt within the confines of object thinking, the only thinking of which we are capable, to transcend this thinking, to go beyond the object with the implements of object thought, to do something indeed without which there can be no philosophy, but which here I can only show in a schema).

The Comprehensive is either the *Being in itself* that surrounds us or the *Being that we are*.

The Being that surrounds us, is called world and transcendence.

The Being that we are is called *dasein*, 'being there', consciousness in general, spirit, existence.

(a) *The Being that surrounds us.*—This being that is, even if we are not, and that surrounds us, but that is not ourselves, is of twofold nature: it is the world, that is to say: the being of which one aspect of our essence constitutes an infinitesimal part, if the world as a whole be considered as something that is not ourselves and in which we are immersed; it is transcendence, that is to say: the being that is intrinsically different from us, in which we have no part, but in which we are rooted and to which we stand in a certain relation.

(aa) *World:* The world as a whole is not an object, but an idea. What we know is in the world, but is never the world.

(bb) *Transcendence:* Transcendence is the being that never becomes world but that speaks as it were through the being that is in the world. There is transcendence only if the world does not consist only of itself, is not built upon itself, but points beyond itself. If the world is everything, then there is no transcendence. But if there is transcendence, perhaps there is something in the world's being that points to it.

(b) *The Being that we are.*—The modes in which we become conscious of our own being are as follows:

(aa) We are *dasein*, being-there. Like all living things we live in an environment. The Comprehensive in this being alive becomes an object of inquiry in its manifestations, in the products of life, in physical forms, in psychological functions, in hereditary morphological contexts, in behaviour patterns, in environmental structures. In addition, man, and only man, produces languages, tools, ideas, acts, in short, he produces himself. All life except for man is merely being-there within its environment. What completes man's being-there is that the following modes of the Comprehensive enter into it, either through man as a vehicle or forced by man into his service.

(bb) We are *consciousness as such* in the division of subject and object. Only what enters into this consciousness is being for us. We are the comprehensive consciousness, in which everything that is can be known, recognized, intended as an object. We break through our mere environment to the idea of the world to which all environments belong, indeed, we think beyond the world, and in our thoughts we can make it disappear as though it were nothing.

(cc) We are *mind*. The life of the mind is the life of

18

ideas. Ideas—for example, the practical idea embodied in our professions and tasks, the theoretical ideas of world, soul, life, etc.—function as impulses in us, as an abstract of the total purpose inherent in the object, as systematic method of penetration, adaptation, and realization, and as such they lead us. They are not objects, but manifest themselves in schemata and forms. They are effective, actual, and at the same time they are infinite tasks.

These three modes of the Comprehensive—being-there, consciousness as such, mind—are the modes in which we are objects in the world; i.e. as this Comprehensive is objectified into a thing that confronts us, we ourselves become adequate empirical objects of biological, psychological, sociological and historical inquiry. But this does not yet exhaust our being.

(dd) We are potential *existence*: We take our life from a primal source that lies beyond the being-there that becomes empirical and objective, beyond consciousness and beyond mind. This aspect of our nature is revealed: (1) in man's experience of *dissatisfaction* with himself, for man feels constantly that he is inadequate to what he is, to his knowledge, his intellectual world; (2) in the *Absolute*, to which he subordinates his empirical existence as to his own authentic selfhood, or as to that which is said to him intelligibly and convincingly; (3) in the unremitting *urge for unity*; for man is not content in one mode of the Comprehensive, or in all modes taken together, but presses toward the fundamental unity which alone is being and eternity; (4) in

19

the consciousness of an indefinable *memory*, as though he shared in the knowledge of creation (Schelling), or as though he remembered something beheld before any world existed (Plato); (5) in the consciousness of *immortality*, that is not a survival in another form, but a time-negating immersion in eternity, appearing to him as a path of action for ever continued in time.

The Comprehensive that I am is in every form a polarity of subject and object:

As *being-there* I am: inner world and environment,

as *consciousness* I am: consciousness and object,

as *mind* I am: the idea that is in me and the objective idea that comes to me from things,

as *existence* I am: existence and transcendence.

The Comprehensive that I am comprehends, as it were, the Comprehensive that Being is and at the same time is comprehended by it. This Being is called 'world' in the first three polarities and then refers to the environment, the objectively intelligible, the idea. In the fourth polarity, it is called 'transcendence'.

Faith in the broadest sense then means presence in these polarities. For this presence can in no event be obtained by the understanding; it always comes from a source of its own, which I cannot will, but through which I will, am and know.

We take the fact of our being-there so for granted that we are not usually aware of the secret that lies in the simple consciousness of reality: I am there, these things are there. Some mental patients temporarily lose their sense of reality. They stamp on the ground, vainly striving to make certain of reality. Everything seems illusory. They feel as if they were dead, they feel like ghosts who are not alive, and, in some grave states of insanity, as if they were doomed to live for ever in this condition of non-living. They call themselves puppets or by some other term indicating unreality. Descartes' *cogito ergo sum* is to be sure an intellectual act, but it cannot give one a sense of reality.

It is as pure consciousness that I experience the truth of a proposition. This evidence is compelling. In every single case, I experience a compelling need to recognize a thing as true or false. But this evidence is always immediate and ultimate.

As mind, I am filled with ideas, through which I capture the idea that confronts me. What is fragmented in the understanding is held together in the mind and becomes an intellectual movement. Where ideas vanish, the world collapses into an infinity of scattered objects.

As existence I am, since I know that I have been given to myself by transcendence. I am not by virtue of my decision alone. Even my freedom, my being-through-myself has been given me. I can be absent from myself and no will can then enable me to give myself to myself.

Now we speak of sense of reality, evidence, idea, as faith in the broader sense. On the level of empirical existence there is something akin to instinct, on the level of pure consciousness there is certainty, on the level of mind there is conviction. But faith proper is the existential act by which transcendence becomes conscious in its actuality.

Faith is life out of the Comprehensive, it is guidance and fulfilment through the Comprehensive.

Faith that springs from the Comprehensive is free, because it is not fixed in any finite thing that has been made into an absolute. It has a character of indetermination (i.e. in reference to what can be stated—I do not know whether and what I believe) and also of the absolute (in practice, in the activity and repose that grow out of the decision).

To speak of it requires the basic philosophical operation, which is to ascertain the Comprehensive by transcending the object within the object thinking that remains for ever inevitable, i.e. to break through the prison of our being that appears to us as split into subject and object, even though we can never really enter into the sphere outside it.

There is something in us that resists this basic operation and thus resists philosophical thought itself. We strive always for something tangible. Hence we erroneously take philosophical ideas for object knowledge. As a cat falls on its four paws, we fall upon the tangible object. We fight against the vertigo of philosophy, against the intimation that we should stand on our heads. We wish to remain 'sane', holding on to our objects and evading the rebirth of our nature in the act of transcending.

But nothing avails. We can retire to the supposed refuge of common sense, but if we try to force everything into its forms, we succumb to the superstition whose essential characteristic is that it freezes into an object, and thus makes tangible, Being itself that transcends any dichotomy of subject and object.

Philosophical faith, with its keen eye for superstition, for faith that is pinned to an object, is consequently incapable of professing dogmatic creeds. The realm of the objective must remain in motion, must evaporate as it were, so that as the object vanishes, a fulfilled consciousness of being is made clear by this very vanishing. Accordingly, philosophical faith is for ever immersed in a dialectical process of fusion and negation.

Dialectic has very diverse meanings. Common to them all is only the essential importance of contradictions. Dialectic means the logical progress through antitheses to a solution in syntheses. Dialectic denotes the movement of reality with its contradictions that tilt into one another, unite, and produce something new. But dialectic also means the exacerbation of antitheses into insoluble antinomies, the fall into the insoluble and the contradictory—it means also a process that leads us to the frontiers where being seems absolutely torn apart, where my authentic being becomes faith, and faith becomes the apprehension of Being in the seemingly absurd.

Philosophical faith contains such dialectical elements.

Just as Being and Nothingness are inseparable, each containing the other, yet each violently repelling the other, so faith and unfaith are inseparable, yet passionately repel one another.

The contradictions of empirical existence, the mind, the world, are reconciled in a harmonious total vision, and the vision is shattered by existential revolt against this untruth.

Faith withdraws to a minimum at the borders of unfaith, and from this infinitesimal point, it reverses the process and spreads anew: thus can I compress myself in my own shrinking self—in the *cogito ergo sum*—; in the pride of inner integrity; *si fractus illabitur orbis, impavidum ferient ruinae*—; in the lifeless attitude of the onlooker: such is life—; in annihilating condemnation of the world ('they can have my ticket back'). In each case I deceive myself into believing that I still exist even when I have no desire to be anything definite, as though it were possible for me to exist outside of the conditions imposed by the finiteness of the world. Through my experience of Nothingness, indeed inspired only by this extreme experience, I once again, with new faith, sail into the open, and begin once more to elucidate all the modes of the Comprehensive which I am and in which I find myself.

It is true that philosophical faith passes through Nothingness, but it is not without roots. It does not begin from scratch, even though it goes back to the primal source. Why do you believe?—Because my father told me. *Mutatis mutandis*, this answer of Kierkegaard applies also to philosophy.

Philosophical faith is in *tradition*. To be sure, this

faith exists only in the independent thinking of each individual, it does not offer the shelter of an objective institution, it is what remains when everything else collapses, and yet it is nothing if one tries to cling to it as a practical support in the world. But always man conquers it by coming to himself, and this he does through tradition. Hence philosophy is determined by its history, and the history of philosophy is rounded out by the philosophizing of each period. . . .

Nowhere at any time has a *philosophia perennis* been achieved, and yet such a philosophy always exists in the idea of philosophical thought and in the general picture of the truth of philosophy considered as its history over three millennia which become a single present.

The question is indeed raised—particularly in view of the achievements of the religions: Does philosophy help man in distress? The question is asked by those who seek an objective, tangible support. But in philosophy there is no such support. The support offered by philosophy is reflection, a gathering of spiritual sustenance through the actualization of the Comprehensive, to win oneself by being given to oneself. Philosophical faith sees itself as exposed, without safeguard or shelter.

And yet the tradition of philosophy is something like a support. The reality of past philosophical thought, of the great philosophers, of the works of philosophy stands before our eyes. Despite our love for particular philosophers through their work, we can never see in a man any more than a man, we must everywhere perceive errors and limits and failures. Even the highest tradition is bound to time, gives neither security nor real fellowship; it cannot become a collection of sacred books, and it knows no work which is valid under all circumstances. Nowhere is the truth ready made; it is an inexhaustible stream that flows from the history of philosophy as a whole from China to the West, yet flows only when the primal source is captured for new realizations in the present.

The word 'Philosophy' has become a symbol of our gratitude for the possibility of continued dialogue with this tradition. It has become our linguistic usage to speak of it as of a living person. Cicero and, most impressively of all, Boethius effected this personification.

Philosophical faith venerates traditional philosophy but does not maintain an attitude of obedience to it. It does not look on history as an authority, but as one continuous spiritual struggle.

History has many meanings. How easily philosophy goes astray when it becomes creed, solidifies into dogmas, establishes school curricula, turns tradition into authority, makes heroes of founders of schools, and where it lets the play of dialectic lead it into irresponsibility. Philosophical faith requires coolness and also complete seriousness. Perhaps great ideas have been more often misunderstood than understood. Perhaps, for example, the history of Platonism (beginning with Speusippus) is a history of perversions and oblivions with but rare moments of rediscovery. Through philosophy men have, contrary to the spirit of philosophy, found the road to nihilism. And so philosophy is held to be dangerous. Not infrequently it is even held to be impossible.

Only through philosophical faith, which always goes back to the primal source, is always capable of recognizing itself in the other, can the road be found through the tangle of aberrations in the history of philosophy to the truth that has dawned in it.

Chapter Two

CONTENTS OF PHILOSOPHICAL
FAITH

FROM PHILOSOPHY ONE tends to expect compelling rational insight, something the truth of which everyone must see and then can know, without any need to believe.

Actually philosophy invokes no revelation and authority. But what the man engaged in philosophical thinking knows through his reason, is far more than compelling intellectual knowledge. It is what from an inner source he apprehends as true, and actualizes with all the organs of his being.

In philosophizing man breaks through his mere nature, but by virtue of his own inner being. What he thus apprehends as Being and as himself, that is his faith. In philosophizing, we travel the path to the primal source of the faith that is the prerogative of man as man.

Rudimentary philosophical ideas come to every man, and it is sometimes in children that they occur in their purest state. To find such thoughts, to clarify and develop them and to repeat them in the recognition of what has been thought through the millennia, is the business of philosophy taken as the professional pursuit of thinking. To this belongs first a methodical reflection on the *area of the contents of faith*, second, reflections on the *contents of faith themselves*.

We have attempted the first. I shall repeat it briefly in a different form.

1. THE AREA OF THE CONTENTS

We are led into the area by four questions: What do I know?—What is authentic?—What is truth?—How do I know?—With the help of the concepts developed in the first lecture, we shall give answers:

First question: What do I know? The answer is: Everything I know falls within the subject-object dichotomy, it is object for me, it is phenomenon, not a thing in itself. But in the subject-object dichotomy object and subject are bound together. There can be no object without a subject, but neither can there be a subject without an object. Hence what I experience as being resides always in the whole of the subject-object dichotomy, not only in one term.

The subject-object dichotomy has many facets: Being-there is within its world which is the environment; consciousness as such is confronted by objects; the mind lives in ideas. Existence stands in relation to transcendence. But environment, ideas, transcendence become objects of cognition only in consciousness through the objectivization in schemata and symbols.

What I know is therefore always object consciousness and hence limited; but though finite, it is a possible springboard toward transcendence.

Second question: What is authentic? The answer is sought and found not by listing the many types of the existent that occur, but by apprehending that which is in itself, or is authentic. Since our inquiry always takes place within the subject-object dichotomy, but since being must transcend or comprehend subject and object, the question of being also bears upon the questioner. The answer must show what being is for us inseparably from what we ourselves are; for being must make possible the inquiry into it through the nature of our own being, and it must be accessible to this inquiry.

There are certain typical answers (some half apt and some utterly fallacious) to the question of Being. First of all, things existing as objects in the world were taken for Being or for the foundation of all the existent: matter, spatial orders, world systems. Being is object.

Conversely the *subjective* was regarded as the source of all being, which it created and objectified. Being is a product of the I.

Purified of the accidents of material determination, being came finally to be conceived as the *thought structures* (categories), which permit us to apprehend all being, because they lie within being itself. In this thinking that is inherent in being, it becomes immediately certain that being is, is not, becomes, is present, is substance, cause and effect, etc. Being is the logos.

The inadequacy of any such ontology points to the specific traits of the philosophical inquiry into being:

(1) If that which authentically is, is not an object, that is, not an object for a subject, then it is beyond cognition, which denotes object knowledge of something.

But since everything that is an object for us reveals to us its phenomenality in contrast to its being-in-itself, phenomenal being points to authentic being, which speaks and is perceptible through it.

(2) If authentic being *is not experience* as subject for a focal point of consciousness observing it, then it also evades all psychological knowledge.

But since being is present in everything that is experienced, the subjective mode of being-there is a basic manifestation of being: experience and understanding are indispensable for the ascertainment of being.

(3) If authentic being is not the *thought structure* of the categories, not logos, it also evades logical knowledge.

But since everything that is for us must enter into some mode of thought, knowledge of the categories is a necessary condition of philosophical clarity.

The authentic being, that is neither object nor subject, but that is manifested in the whole of the subject-object dichotomy, and that must fill the categories in order to give them purpose and meaning, we have called the Comprehensive.

The question of authentic being must therefore find its answer through elucidation of the modes of the Comprehensive—of world and transcendence—of being-there, consciousness, mind, existence. But in so far as all these modes are rooted in one, the ultimate answer is that authentic being is transcendence (or God), a proposition the true understanding of which embraces all philosophical faith and all elucidating philosophical thought, but the path to which leads through all the modes of the Comprehensive.

Third question: What is truth? Answer: In every mode of the Comprehensive that we are, a specific meaning of truth is rooted.

In being-there resides truth as the immediacy of the sensibly actual, as vital utility, as instinct, as the practical and the opportune.

In consciousness resides truth as the freedom from contradiction of that which is thinkable as object in the universal categories.

In the mind resides truth as conviction of ideas.

In existence resides truth as authentic faith. Faith is the consciousness of existence in reference to transcendence.

All truth is expressed in the medium of consciousness, which however provides only formal truth, whereas the source of truth is to be sought in the other modes of the Comprehensive.

Fourth question: How do I know? When doubt puts in an appearance, I seek foundations. I ask how I know, I inquire into the meaning and limits of this knowledge. Then it becomes clear that all truth is apprehended in a specific mode of thought. We become conscious of these modes of thought through the study of the categories and of methodology, which provide a basic framework of philosophical thought. Thus I am enabled not only to know, but to know how and by what means I know.

For one wishing to philosophize, it is of particular, indeed of crucial importance to ascertain the difference between the object cognition that is achieved in the sciences, and the transcending thought that characterizes philosophy. A philosophical discussion may be said to have reached its goal when the matter under discussion becomes objectless, in the double sense that for the positivist nothing remains to be done, because he no longer sees an object, and that for the philosopher the light is just beginning to dawn. The philosopher cannot to be sure apprehend authentic being in the vanishing of the object, but he can be filled by it.

Our four questions result in intellectual operations which transcend the limits of the knowable and of the world as a whole, so that through these limits we become aware of the phenomenality of empirical existence and hence of the Comprehensive nature of being, thus entering into the area of faith. This transcendent thinking is a thinking that through method acquires a scientific character and yet, because in it the determinate object is dissolved, differs from scientific cognition.

These intellectual operations do not carry compelling evidence like empiric and rational insights into finite objects, but they have a compelling character for him who performs them, who in them transcending the finite, gains awareness of the infinite through the finite.

Since he moves in the area of the limit, he inevitably becomes aware of the limit as such; using categories, he methodically transcends these same categories; in non-knowledge he finds a new mode of objectless knowledge. This philosophizing carries out intellectual operations which do not yet reveal any contents of faith, but do pave the way for them.

2. CONTENTS OF FAITH

The contents of philosophical faith can be stated in such propositions as the following:

God is.

There is an absolute imperative.

The world is an ephemeral stage between God and existence.

(1) *God is:* Transcendence beyond the world or before the world is called God. There is the profoundest difference whether I regard the universe as being in itself and nature as God, or whether I regard the universe as not grounded in itself and find the foundation of the world and myself in something outside the world.

We have the proofs for the existence of God. Since Kant, honest thinkers are agreed that such proofs are impossible if they aim to compel the intellect, as one can compel it to realize that the earth revolves around the sun and that the moon has a reverse side. But the arguments for the existence of God do not lose their validity as ideas because they have lost their power to prove. They amount to a confirmation of faith by in-

intellectual operations. When they are original, the thinker struck by their evidence experiences them as the profoundest event of life. When they are reflected upon with understanding, they make possible a repetition of this experience. The idea as such effects a transformation in man, it opens our eyes, in a sense. More than that, it becomes a fundament of ourselves, by enhancing our awareness of being, it becomes the source of personal depth.

The arguments for the existence of God start from something that can be found and experienced in the world, to arrive at the conclusion: if this is, then God must exist. Thus the fundamental mysteries of the cosmos are brought to awareness as stepping stones to God.

Or one performs intellectual operations in which thinking is understood as awareness of Being, which then is deepened into an awareness of God: this is speculative philosophy proper.

Or the presence of God is ascertained existentially: the distinction between good and evil is viewed in its full import as a commandment of God. God speaks in the reality of love.

And in every case, the presence of gaps in the world structure, the failure of all attempts to conceive of the world as self-contained, the abortion of human planning, the futility of human designs and realizations, the impossibility of fulfilling man himself brings us to the edge of the abyss, where we experience nothingness or God.

But never do we gain a scientifically cogent proof. A proved God is no God. Accordingly: only he who starts from God, can seek him. A certainty of the existence of God, however rudimentary and intangible it may be, is a premise, not a result of philosophical activity.

Since Kant's magnificent confutation of all arguments for the existence of God, since the brilliant but comfortable and false restoration of these proofs by Hegel, since the revived interest in the medieval proofs, a philosophical reformulation of the arguments for the existence of God has become an urgent necessity. Theodor Haubach, the socialist and conspirator of the July 20th uprising, who was hanged by the Gestapo— this political thinker and realist, inspired by hope in the new Germany to be built after the certain collapse, took a deep interest during the war years in the arguments for God's existence, which he looked upon as an indispensable foundation for the consciousness that would unite us all.

The thought that God is, is directly followed by speculation as to what he is. This is impossible to discover, and yet speculation on it has unfolded rich, inspiring thoughts. The field, to be sure, is held by the negative theology that tells us what God is not—to wit, he is not something that stands in finite form before the eyes or the mind. But finite things serve as metaphor, symbol, analogy, enabling us to realize the presence of the divine.

(2) *There is an absolute imperative:* In general the im-

36

peratives that are addressed to us, are based upon practical aims, or upon an unquestioned authority. Such imperatives are determined by the aim or by blind obedience.

An absolute imperative has its source within me, in that it sustains me. Neither finite aims nor authority can account for this absolute. That the absolute exists as a foundation for action is not a matter of cognition, but an essential element of faith. Our finite thinking is always relative and thus can in some way justify everything. The apprehension of the absolute has, in the historicity of our here and now, an infinite character; although it is elucidated in universal propositions, it cannot be adequately defined and derived through any universal.

The absolute imperative confronts me as the command of my authentic self to my empirical existence, as the command as it were of what I am eternally in the face of the transcendent, to the temporality of my present life. If my will is grounded in the absolute, I apprehend it as that which I myself authentically am, and to which my empirical existence should correspond.

The Absolute itself does not become temporal. Wherever it is, it cuts straight across time. It erupts from the Transcendent into this world by way of our freedom.

(3) *The reality of the world subsists ephemerally between God and existence:* The indeterminate character of all modes of known reality, the interpretive character of all cognition, the fact that we apprehend all being in the

dichotomy of subject and object—these essential characteristics of the knowledge that is possible for us mean that all objects are mere phenomena, that no being that is the object of cognition is being in itself and the whole of being. The phenomenality of the empirical world is a basic insight of philosophical thought. This insight is not empirical; it can be attained only by an act of transcendence; on the other hand, it imposes itself on every intellect that is capable of transcendence. It does not add a new particular item of knowledge to previous knowledge, but effects a shift in the whole consciousness of being. Hence the sudden but permanent light that dawns upon one after a more or less prolonged study of Kant. The student of Kant who fails to experience this revelation has not understood his teachings, has bogged down in a doctrine of which he does not realize the ultimate implication.

The world as a whole does not become an object for us. Every object is in the world, none is the world. Any definition or judgment of the world, whether it be an optimistic affirmation or a pessimistic negation of the universal harmony, leads to generalizations which give preference to some realities at the expense of others. If we reject such generalizations, we realize that the world is not self-contained, that it is not grounded in itself, and we become willing to open ourselves permanently to all the modes of the world's being, to what happens outside ourselves and to what we ourselves have done in the temporal course of life. Such willingness is bound up with:

First, recognition of the absolute transcendence of God in relation to the world: the *deus absconditus* recedes into the distance when I seek to fathom him, he is infinitely near in the absolute historicity of the unique situation—and the situation is always unique.

Secondly, the experience of the world as the language of God: the world has no independent existence, in it is manifested the speech of God, a speech that has always many meanings and that can become historically unequivocal for existence only in the evanescent moment.

For such faith our being in time is an encounter of existence and transcendence—of the eternal that we are, as beings that are both created and self-given—and of the eternal in itself. The world is the meeting point of that which is eternal and that which manifests itself in time.

But since the encounter between existence and transcendence is an encounter in the world, it is bound to the world from the standpoint of time. Because what is for us, must manifest itself within the temporality of the world, there is no direct knowledge of God and existence. The study of the world is our only road to knowledge, self-realization in the world is the only road to existential self-realization. If we are lost to the world, we are also lost to ourselves.

Of these propositions expressing the substance of faith it can be said:

None is demonstrable in the same sense as finite knowledge. Their truth can be shown only by calling

39

attention to them, by following their line of thought, or by remembering their substance. They remain in the uncertain realm of non-knowledge.

One feels a certain diffidence about giving a clear statement of articles of faith. When clearly stated, they are too readily treated like knowledge and then they lose their meaning. They beguile him who states them to raising false claims.

But I am compelled to make a direct statement in philosophizing, for here the questions arise: Is there God? Is empirical existence subject to an absolute law? Is the world the ultimate, or is it precarious and ephemeral?

The propositions of unfaith are:

First: there is no God, for there is only the world and the laws of nature; the world is God.

Second: there is no absolute, for the commandments that I follow came into being and are conditioned by habit, practice, tradition, obedience; everything is relative *ad infinitum*.

Third: the world is everything, the sole and authentic reality. Everything in the world is indeed transient, but the world itself is absolute, eternal, not ephemeral, not suspended in transition.

In philosophizing, non-knowledge should not be invoked as a pretext for evading all answers. I do not know whether I believe. But faith takes hold of me to such an extent that I dare to live by it. While the philosopher's statements may remain indeterminate and suggest indecision, his actual attitude in a historical situation is one of resolution. This tension characterizes philosophy.

The essential philosophical themes of Western philosophy have their historical source not only in Greek, but in Biblical thought as well. Those who cannot believe in revelation as such, can nevertheless make the Biblical source their own, letting themselves be permeated by its human truth, without revelation. The study of the Bible has indeed been one of the foundations of nearly all Western philosophy up till to-day. This unique work belongs to no one denomination or religion, but to all.

We become aware of our specific roots in Biblical religion when we compare it to Indian and East Asiatic religions. True, the fundamental characteristics of Biblical religion are not entirely lacking in the other religions, but here they do not permeate the whole structure. Even in the Bible these fundamental characteristics are not everywhere; some of them are to be found only in a few passages, but these passages are uniquely effective. Let me recall these fundamental traits:

(1) *The one God:* The One becomes the foundation of consciousness of being and ethos, the source of active immersion in the world. No other gods beside God, that is the metaphysical foundation for the serious striving for the One in the world.

(2) *The transcendence of the God-Creator:* The conquest of the daemonic world and of magic brings to consciousness the transcendence of the imageless, formless,

unthinkable God. The idea of creation brings the world as a whole into a state of suspension. The world is not grounded in itself, and does not originate in itself. Man as an individual in existence achieves his freedom in the world through being created by God; in his bond with the transcendent God, and only by virtue of this bond, is he independent of the world.

(3) *Encounter of man with God:* The transcendent God has a personal aspect. He is a person, to whom man turns. There is a striving toward God, a striving to hear God, and out of it grows a passionate personal quest for God's personality. Biblical religion is a religion of prayer. Prayer in its pure form—free from worldly desires—is praise and thanksgiving and ends in the trustful: 'Thy will be done.'

(4) *God's commandments:* With a unique simplicity, fundamental truths are expressed in the ten commandments as commandments of God. The difference between good and evil is conceived as an absolute either/or. Since the days of the prophets, charity is enjoined, culminating in the maxim: 'Love thy neighbour as thyself.'

(5) *Sense of historicity:* This appears in the epoch of political catastrophes as a universal historical consciousness of a history guided by God. It becomes the foundation of the religiocentric life that draws the whole universe into the here and now. Life is no longer endlessly fragmented and accidental; God-sustained actuality invests it with its full significance.

(6) *Suffering:* Suffering achieves dignity, suffering be-

comes a road to godhead. In the story of the servant of God (Deutero-Isaiah) and in the symbol of the Cross (Christ) it becomes the antithesis of the Greek tragic principle. Biblical religion lives outside or beyond the sense of the tragic.

(7) *Openness to the insoluble:* The certitude of faith exposes itself to the utmost trials. It dares to disclose the insoluble that grows out of given religious positions—and every statement becomes inevitably a position. The impassioned struggle with God for God is uniquely revealed in Job. Nihilistic despair—seen as a transitional stage which the man of integrity cannot evade—is given unequalled expression in Ecclesiastes.

Each of these fundamental traits is subject to specific distortions.

(1) *The one God becomes abstract* and then remains only a negative principle opposed to the world, to its multiplicity and plenitude. The One kills the Many.

(2) The *transcendent God* detaches himself from the world. God without creation is an idea in which everything vanishes. As the world becomes not only vain, but void, we are led to reduce transcendence also to nothingness, as it were, and so nothing is left.

(3) The *meeting with* God is interpreted in a selfish or sentimental sense. This religion of prayer holds the danger of an egocentric importuning of God.

Another danger is the tendency to imagine that God's will can be known with certainty; this becomes a source of fanaticism. Many of the horrible things done in the world have been justified by God's will. Fanatics fail to hear the many meanings inherent in every experience of God's voice. Any one who knows for certain what God says and wants, makes God into a being in the world, over which he disposes, and is thus on the road to superstition. But no worldly claim or justification can be based upon the voice of God. What is solid certainty in the individual and sometimes can become so for a community, cannot be concretely formulated in terms of universal validity.

(4) *God's commandments* are transformed from simple foundations of morality into abstract juridical propositions and develop into an infinity of particular rulings.

(5) The sense of *historicity* is perverted into a conception of history as a process independent of man. Then man imagines that he is the master of history, whether intellectually in a knowledge of the whole, or actively, in the conviction that he is familiar with the divine plan and is carrying it out. Or there arises an æsthetic conception, in which man makes light of his own existence as against history as a whole.

(6) *Suffering,* through psychological transpositions becomes masochistic pleasure or is sadistically approved, or it is conceived as a sacrifice in outdated magical categories.

(7) Openness to the *insoluble* leads to despair or nihilism, to the revolt of a boundless negation.

Up to our own day Biblical religion has given rise to such aberrations. The savagery that not infrequently appears in it, is a sort of perversion of the original pathos of faith. The old religious impulse still has compelling force, and when men translate its aberrations into practice, the result is a hideous combination of vital urges and their perversions.

3. REASON AND COMMUNICATION

Reference to the realm of the Comprehensive, and to a number of propositions which state the essential themes of faith but nevertheless remain indeterminate, is not sufficient to characterize philosophical faith. For essentially philosophical thinking takes place in time. Philosophy is a transition between origin and goal. Something in us that leads us along this road, some subjective drive or compulsion and objective attraction, though it is itself nothing tangible, something through which we really have philosophical life, is called reason. Reason is never without intelligence, but it is infinitely more than intelligence. Reason is an indispensable element of philosophical faith. All other truth-meanings become clearly visible only when they are decanted in the movement of reason. Let us characterize reason:

Reason relates all the various meanings of truth to one another, by asserting each one. It prevents any truth from being confined to itself. It understands that any faith which isolates and hypostatizes one mode of the Comprehensive, is false. Thus for example, even the 'faith' of consciousness errs when it maintains that being is free from contradiction. For pure consciousness can only go so far as to say that what does not accord with its principles, the law of contradiction, for example, is beyond its grasp. But even the total contents accessible to the pure consciousness are not yet being itself, but only the mode of its manifestation in the categories of universally valid thought.

Reason forbids fixation in any truth-meaning that does not embrace all truth. It forbids resignation, it forbids us to lose ourselves in blind alleys, it forbids us to content ourselves with limited solutions, however seductive, it forbids us to forget or pass anything by, whether it is reality or value or possibility. Reason urges us to leave nothing out of account, to relate ourselves with everything that is, to seek beyond all limits what is and should be, to encompass even antinomies, and always apprehend the whole, to apprehend every possible harmony.

But then again reason strives to effect the necessary break-through in every totality. It forbids definitive harmony. It goes to the extreme to apprehend authentic being.

Its root is not a destructive will, such as is manifested in the relativism of intellectual sophistry, but openness to the infinity of meaningful contents. To doubt is imperative to it, but it doubts in order to gain pure truth. The understanding, as unanchored thought, is nihilistic; reason, as grounded in existence, is salvation from nihilism, because it preserves the confidence that through its movement in conjunction with the understanding, it will, amid the conflicts, divisions, and abysses of the concrete world, regain in the end its certitude of transcendence.

Reason is the Comprehensive in us; it does not flow from the primal source of being, but is an instrument of existence. It is the existential absolute that serves to actualize the primal source and bring it to the widest manifestation.

There is something like a climate of reason. The passion for the open works in cool clarity. The rational man lives resolutely out of the root of his own historical soil, and at the same time he gives himself to every mode of historicity which he encounters, in order to penetrate to the depth of the world's historicity, through which alone a sympathetic understanding of everything becomes possible. From this develops what was also the motive force from the outset—the love of being, of everything existent as existent in its transparency, thanks to which its relations to the primal source become visible. Reason enriches man by sharpening his hearing, increases his capacity for communication, makes him capable of change through new experience, but while doing all this it remains essentially one, unswerving in its faith, living in actually efficacious memory of everything that was once real to it.

He who engages in philosophy cannot sufficiently praise reason, to which he owes all his achievements. Reason is the bond that unites all the modes of the Comprehensive. It allows no existent to separate itself absolutely, to sink into isolation, to be reduced to nothingness by fragmentation. Nothing must be lost.

Where reason is effective, that which is strives for uni-
fication. A universal fellowship arises, in which men
are open to all things and everything concerns them.
Reason quickens dormant springs, frees what is hidden,
makes possible authentic struggles. It presses toward
the One that is all, it does away with the delusions that
fixate the One prematurely, incompletely, in partisan-
ship.

Reason demands boundless *communication*, it is itself
the total will to communicate. Because, in time, we
cannot have objective possession of a truth that is the
eternal truth, and because being-there is possible only
with other being-there, and existence can come into its
own only with other existence, communication is the
form in which truth is revealed in time.

The great seductions are: through belief in God to
withdraw from men; through supposed knowledge of
the absolute truth to justify one's isolation; through
supposed possession of being itself to fall into a state
of complacency that is in truth lovelessness. And to
these may be added the assertion that every man is a
self-contained monad, that no one can emerge from
himself, that communication is a delusion.

In opposition to these stands philosophical faith,
which may also be called faith in communication. For
it upholds these two propositions: Truth is what joins
us together; and, truth has its origin in communication.
The only reality with which man can reliably and in
self-understanding ally himself in the world, is his
fellow man. At all the levels of communication among

men, companions in fate lovingly find the road to the truth. This road is lost to the man who shuts himself off from others in stubborn self-will, who lives in a shell of solitude.

Chapter Three

MAN

THE GIGANTIC TOPIC of 'man' can barely be touched upon in an hour's time. Since we are men, it is assuredly of the utmost importance for us to know of man. We are even told: To know what man is, is the only knowledge that is possible for us, for we are men ourselves—and that alone is essential —for man is the measure of all things. One can speak of all other things only in relation to man, that is, one can speak only of what he encounters in the world, of what serves him, and of what is beyond his powers. What he sees, hears, touches, has for him the characteristic of real actuality. Whatever else he has in his thoughts, is his imagining, produced by him. If we confine ourselves to man, we shall have what is accessible to us, what concerns us; we shall have everything that is.

For a moment this sounds convincing and yet it is replete with fallacy. It is indeed true that everything that is manifests itself to us in such a way that we can apprehend it. Hence the great postulate that all being become actual for man, that he experience it, that he

receive it in his here and now. This postulate is a fundamental characteristic of humanity; witness the extraordinary fact that infinitesimal man, a nothing in a tiny
corner of the infinite universe, in his narrow space, is
concerned with what stands beyond and before the
existence of the world. Valid for him is only what
becomes present for him. After writing his famous
words about the starry heavens above me and the moral
law within me, Kant continues: 'These two things I
may not do . . . seek beyond my sphere and merely
presume; I see them before me and link them immediately with the consciousness of my existence. The
first begins at the place that I occupy in the outward
sensory world. . . . The second begins with my invisible
self . . . and represents me in a world . . . with which I
know myself to stand not in a mere accidental relation
as with that other world, but in a universal and
necessary context. . . .'

But though what is must become actual for man,
since for him all being lies in presence, it is not brought
forth by man; man produces neither sensible realities,
nor the content of his ideas, his thoughts and symbols.
What really is, is even without man, even though it
appears to us in forms and modes that originate in man.
Indeed, we have better knowledge of all those things
that we ourselves are not—what man is, is perhaps less
clear to him than anything else he encounters. He becomes for himself the greatest of all mysteries when he
senses that despite his finite nature, his possibilities
seem to extend into the infinite.

Man defined himself first by means of great images, as though he already understood himself: First he conceived of himself in the hierarchy of the creatures. As a sensual being, he is the highest of the beasts, as a spiritual being, the lowest of the angels; yet he is neither beast nor angel, but related to both by a part of his nature, superior to each by virtue of that which is lacking in one or the other, but which he possesses from his own origin, as the direct creation of God.

Or man is conceived as the microcosm which contains everything that the world, the macrocosm, enfolds. Man corresponds to no other being, only to the world as a whole. This idea was developed in detail and graphically illustrated by specific correspondences between man's organs and cosmic phenomena. Aristotle expressed it sublimely and profoundly when he said: The soul is in a certain sense everything.

Secondly, man's being was seen in his situation rather than in the image of his form. The fundamental human situation in which he finds himself, is at the same time the fundamental characteristic of his being:

Bede tells of the Anglo-Saxon council summoned to decide on the question of the acceptance of the Christian faith in 627. One of the dukes compared the life of man on earth with the flight of a sparrow through a banquet hall in winter,[1] 'a good fire in the midst, whilst the storms of rain and snow prevail abroad; the sparrow, I say, flying in at one door, and immediately out

[1] Bede the Venerable, *Ecclesiastical History of the English Nation* (London 1916), p. 91.

at another, whilst he is within, is safe from the wintry storm; but after a short space of fair weather, he immediately vanishes out of your sight, into the dark winter from which he had emerged. So this life of man appears for a short space, but of what went before, or what is to follow we are utterly ignorant.' This Germanic heathen feels himself dependent on something alien, he feels that he is here in the world by accident, but in this life he feels happy and sheltered; his care is for the brevity of life and for what comes after.

Like him, St. Augustine (*de beata vita*) sees the mystery of man's entrance into this life, but with an opposite value judgment: 'For since God or nature or necessity or our will, or all together—the matter is very obscure—seemingly unthinking and at random has cast us into this world as into a stormy sea. . . .'

Thirdly, man's being has been seen in his misery and greatness at once, in his weakness and potentiality, in the mystery of how his opportunities and tasks develop precisely out of his fragility. This image of man runs in modulations through all Western history:

The Greeks knew that no man is to be called happy before his death. He is exposed to an uncertain fate; men pass away, like the leaves in the forest. To forget the measure of man is hybris, the ensuing fall is all the more precipitate. But the Greeks also knew that: There are many mighty things, but nothing mightier than man.

The Old Testament knows the same polarity. It expresses the nothingness of man:

As for man, his days are as grass,
As a flower of the field, so he flourisheth.
For the wind passeth over it, and it is gone,
And the place thereof shall know it no more.

Psalm ciii, 15, 16.

But man's greatness is also seen:

For thou hast made him a little lower than the angels,
And hast crowned him with glory and honour.
Thou madest him to have dominion over the works of thy
hands;
Thou hast put all things under his feet.

Psalm viii, 5. 6.

But exalted above this conception of man's fragility and greatness, which is common to many peoples, is the Old Testament conception of man as the likeness of the godhead: God created man in His image. Man fell from God and now embodies both the likeness to God, and sin.

The Christians continued on this road. So definite was their knowledge of man's limitation that they found it even in the man-god: In the deepest torment Jesus experienced what he expressed on the Cross in the words of the Psalm: My God, my God, why hast thou forsaken me? Man cannot stand on himself.

This candid view of man's limitation permits the Christians in their legends to look upon even the holiest of men as capable of despair and guilt. Peter, questioned by the maid and in fear of the executioners, thrice

54

denied Jesus. Rembrandt painted this man (the paint-
ing, now in Leningrad, was for a time on exhibit in
Holland): Peter's face at the moment of his denial,
unforgettably revealing a basic trait of our human
nature; the menacing executioners; the furious, trium-
phant maid; the mild gaze of Jesus in the background.

St. Paul and St. Augustine understood the impossibility of the good man being really good. Why can he
not be really good? When he does a good deed, he must
know that he is doing a good deed; but this very knowledge is self-satisfaction and therefore pride. Without
self-reflection there can be no human goodness, with
self-reflection the goodness cannot be blameless and
pure.

Pico della Mirandola, in the joy of the still Christian
Renaissance, portrayed man in accord with the idea of
him outlined by God when He put him into the world
at the end of the creation: God made man in his image,
combining in him all things, and said to him: We have
given thee no definite dwelling-place, no particular
heritage. We have subordinated all other beings in
creation to definite laws. Thou alone art in nothing
restricted and canst take upon thyself and choose to be
what thou wilt. Thou thyself, according to thy will and
thy glory, shalt be thine own masterworker and sculp-
tor and form thyself of the stuff that is to thy liking.
Thus thou art free to descend to the lowest level of
the animal world. But thou canst also raise thyself to
the highest spheres of godhead.—The animals possess
from birth everything they will ever possess. In man

alone God scattered the seeds of every action and the germs of every kind of life.

Pascal, tormented by the Christian sense of sin, saw both the greatness and the misery of man. Man is everything and he is nothing. With no ground beneath his feet, he stands between two infinites. Composed of irreconcilable opposites, he lives in insatiable unrest, he is neither a reconciled middle term, nor a complacent mediocrity. 'What a chimera is man! What a monster, what a chaos, what a thing of contradiction . . . judger of all things, foolish earthworm . . . glory and excrement of the universe. . . . Man infinitely transcends man. . . . Unhappy as we are we have an idea of happiness, and we cannot attain it. We carry within us an image of the truth and possess only error. We are incapable of absolute ignorance and of certain knowledge.'

But we have given enough historical examples of the conception of man's nature. Let us now attempt to achieve fundamental clarity concerning the knowledge of man. There are two ways of looking at man; either as an object of inquiry, or as freedom.

Man is an object of inquiry for anatomy, physiology, psychology and sociology. Anthropology—ethnology and morphology—studies his physical existence as a whole. We have acquired a considerable body of knowledge, the basic feature of which is that all its insights, even the relative generalizations, are particular; the insights remain scattered, do not combine into a complete system. Consequently this knowledge of man always goes astray when it leads to total judgments on man, to supposed understanding of the whole.

Of essential philosophical importance are the fundamental questions. The question of the difference between man and beast (and with it the question of man's origin) is perhaps the most interesting question of all. Here we have possibilities of empirical investigation, while an inquiry into the difference between man and angel can only be carried on in imaginative constructions which—though instructive—measure man by hypothetical potentialities.

Two contradictory basic experiences are the points of departure of scientific investigation. We see ourselves as a link in the chain of living things, one among many. The question of the difference between man and animal has become misleading. I can only propound a definite and answerable question concerning the difference, for example, between man and ape, between the ape and other animals, etc., but I cannot inquire into the difference between man and animal.

The other experience is: We see man's body in its incomparable expression. It belongs to man himself, has its own unique specificity, its nobility and beauty, in comparison to which every other living thing seems particular, as though moving down a blind alley. Even in man's body we seek after these incomparable basic traits, and in our comparison place him in opposition to all other living things.

Facts have been disclosed along both lines of approach, but really decisive ones only in the first. Yet answers leading to important fundamental results can be obtained only by following the second approach. If something truly unique were found in the physical structure of man, the first line of investigation would acquire a more specific meaning. Up to now, this has not been done, despite the many answers offered, from the discovery that only man can laugh, to the assertion that the structure of man's body is physiologically and morphologically open, and that in distinction from all other living things that seem to adhere to rigid patterns, his body somehow embraces all the potentialities of the living.—The question of present fact must be distinguished from the question of origin. The latter is involved when man is conceived as an abortive embryonic development or as a phenomenon of domestication through civilization, analogous to the domestic animals—both absurd conceptions. Portmann's epoch-making research into the phenomena of man's early childhood and adolescence has revealed, no doubt for the first time, by biological methods, that even as regards his physical structure man achieves his specifically human characteristics with the help of elements pertaining to historical tradition; in other words, man, including his biological traits, cannot be explained merely by the laws of heredity, but must be placed within a historical framework.

But we are far removed from any certain biological understanding of the uniqueness of man's physical life, although we think we can see it without scientific knowledge.

Closely connected with the question of the difference between man and animal, is the question of man's origin, of how he became man. In this connection, it may be presumed, science will undergo the same experience as in the question of the origin of life in general. The progress of knowledge increases our non-knowledge of the fundamental questions and thus suggests the existence of limits and the need to draw upon sources other than cognition.

Thirty years ago a geologist asked me to deliver a lecture on the origin of life. I replied: The greatness of biology is revealed by the fact that in contrast to earlier unclear conceptions of transitions, it is coming to an increasingly definite realization that this origin is unfathomable. The geologist: But either life must have originated on earth, that is, from the inorganic, or its germs must have flown in from the cosmos. Myself: This looks like a perfect disjunctive proposition, but obviously both alternatives are impossible. The geologist: Then you take refuge in miracles? Myself: No, but in knowledge I seek to gain only the essential non-knowledge. The geologist: That I do not understand. You are pursuing something negative. The world is after all understandable, otherwise our whole science would be meaningless. Myself: But perhaps what gives it meaning is precisely and solely that through understanding it comes up against that which is authentically un-understandable. And perhaps it is meaningful to express the un-understandable through the play of thought at the limit of cognition. To conceive of life germs in the cosmos, flying everywhere, creating life, seems just such a play of thought, because life of this kind has always been. But that is a trivial and meaningless play of thought. It seems to me that a more expressive play is to be found in Preyer's idea that the world is one single gigantic body of life, and that everything that is not alive is its excrement and corpse. Then it is not the origin of life, but the origin of the non-living that would have to be explained.

A similar problem is that of the origin of man. Important material has been contributed, consisting for the most part of hypotheses, but also of some isolated facts. On the whole, the mystery has grown deeper, our vision of prehistory has been somewhat illumined, but the fundament of man's origin has become more and more unfathomable. The best of these impossible conceptions seems to me that of Dacqué: man has always existed, he lived in various animal forms, yet was entirely different from the morphologically related animal forms, from the fish, the reptile, etc. Man, one might continue, has always been the authentic form of life, and all other life is a degeneration from man; in the last analysis, it was not man that developed from ape, but ape from man. And now perhaps we are facing a new and long-term process of regression: perhaps there will come into being a new animal species which will become petrified in a technological mode of life, and beside it a new humanity will develop, from whose vantage point this mass will seem like another species, something that is merely living but is no longer human.

These are far-fetched speculations, and yet they do cast a certain light upon our non-knowledge.

The matter was admirably summed up by a joke that appeared in *Simplicissimus* during the first World War. Two Bavarian peasants are talking things over. People are pretty dumb, says one, maybe Darwin was right after all. Maybe we are descended from the apes.—Yes, says the other, but just the same I'd like to see the ape that first noticed that he wasn't an ape any more.

Man cannot be derived from something else, but is immediately at the base of all things. To be aware of this signifies man's freedom, which is lost in every other total determination of his being, and comes entirely into its own only in this one total determination. All empirical causalities and biological processes of development would seem to apply to man's material substratum, not to himself. No one can tell how far science will advance in the knowledge of the development of this human substratum. And scarcely any field of research is more exciting and captivating.

Every insight into man, if it is absolutized into a supposed knowledge of man as a whole, destroys his freedom. And this is the case with such theories of man, meaningful for limited perspectives, as have been propounded by psychoanalysis, Marxism, racial theory. They veil man himself as soon as they attempt to investigate anything more than aspects of his nature.

Science, it is true, shows us remarkable and highly surprising things about man, but as it attains greater clarity, the more evident it becomes that man as a whole can never become the object of scientific investigation. Man is always more than he knows about himself. This is true both of man in general and of the individual man. We can never draw up a balance sheet and know the answer, either concerning man in general, or concerning any individual man.

To absolutize knowledge that is always particular into a whole knowledge of man leads to the utter neglect of the human image of man. And a neglect of the image of man leads to a neglect of man himself. For the image of man that we hold to be true is itself a factor in our life. It influences our behaviour toward ourselves and others, our vital attitude, and our choice of tasks.

Each of us for himself is certain of what man is, in a way that precedes scientific research and also comes after it. This is the prerogative of our freedom, which knows itself bound up with cogent knowledge, but is not included in it as an object of cognition. For in so far as we make ourselves the object of scientific inquiry, we see no freedom, but factuality, finiteness, form, relation, causal necessity. But it is by our freedom that we have awareness of our humanity.

Let me sum up once again, in order to gain a more secure foundation for our consciousness of freedom.

Man cannot be understood on the basis of evolution from the animals.

In opposition to this we have the thesis: Without such evolution it is impossible to explain his origin. Since this is the only intelligible explanation and since everything in the world takes place in accordance with intelligible laws, man must have come into being through such an evolution.

The answer: True, for our cognition, everything is intelligible, for only where there is intelligibility is there cognition; beyond cognition, nothing exists for cognition. But the whole of being does not by any means resolve into intelligibility, if by cognition we mean scientifically cogent knowledge capable of being communicated, unchanged. This knowledge itself is always particular, it refers always to definite, finite objects—whenever it approaches the whole as such, it slides into fundamental fallacies.

The world as a whole cannot be apprehended on the basis of one or several or many intelligible principles. Cognition breaks it into fragments—after the first erroneous and vain thrust toward the whole. Cognition is in the world and does not comprehend the world. Universal knowledge—as in mathematics and in the natural sciences—does indeed encompass something universal, but never reality as a whole.

But it would be a new fallacy to effect a leap within knowledge to other knowledge. To imagine, for instance, that at the limit of the knowable there is a creator of the world, and to suppose that this creator intervenes in the course of the world. As far as knowledge is concerned, these are merely metaphoric tautologies for non-knowledge.

The world is disclosed as having no foundation in itself. But in himself man finds what he finds nowhere else in the world: something unknowable, undemonstrable, something that is never object, that evades all scientific inquiry: he finds freedom and what goes with it. In this sphere I have experience not through knowledge of something, but through action. Here the road leads through the world and ourselves to transcendence.

To those who deny it freedom cannot be proved like things that occur in the world. But since the primal source of our action and our consciousness of being lies in freedom, what man is, is not merely the object of knowledge, but also of *faith*. Man's certainty as to his humanity is one of the basic elements of philosophical faith.

But man's freedom is inseparable from his *consciousness of his finite nature*.

Let us briefly outline the main points: Man's finiteness is first of all the finiteness of all living things. He is dependent upon his environment, upon nourishment and sensory contents; he is inexorably exposed to the mute and blind natural process; he must die.

Man's finiteness is secondly his dependence on other men, and on the historical world produced by the human collectivity. He can rely on nothing in this world. The fruits of fortune come and go. The human order is ruled not only by justice, but also by the power of the moment, that declares its arbitrary will to be the organ of justice, and hence is always based partly upon untruth. State and national community can destroy men who work for them all their lives. Reliance can be placed only on the loyalty of man in existential communication, but this cannot be calculated. For what one relies on here is not an objective, demonstrable reality. And the man closest to one can at any time fall sick, go mad, die.

Man's finiteness lies thirdly in the nature of his cognition, in his dependence on the experience that is given him, especially on direct perception. My intellect can apprehend nothing but the matter of direct perception that fills in my concept.

Man becomes conscious of his finiteness by comparison with something that is not finite, with the absolute and the infinite:

The *absolute* becomes actual for him in his decision, the fulfilment of which directs him to an origin other than that which science makes intelligible to him in his finite existence.

The *infinite* is touched, though not apprehended, first in the idea of infinity, then in the conception of a divine knowledge essentially different from man's finite knowledge, finally in thoughts of immortality. The infinite which though unfathomable does enter into man's consciousness, causes man to transcend his finiteness by becoming aware of it.

Through the presence of the absolute and the infinite, man's finiteness does not remain merely the unconscious datum of his empirical existence; but through the light of transcendence it becomes the basic trait in his consciousness of his created nature. Thus though man cannot annul his finiteness, he does break through it.

But if in the absoluteness of his decision in the face of everything finite in the world, he becomes through his independence, certain of his infinity as his authentic selfhood, this infinity also reveals a new mode of his finiteness. This finiteness as existence means that even as himself man cannot ascribe himself to himself. It is not through himself that he is originally himself. And just as he does not owe his empirical existence in the world to his own will, his self is a free gift to him by transcendence. He must be given to himself over and over again, if he is not to lose himself. If man maintains his inner integrity in the face of fate and even of death, he cannot do so by himself alone. What helps him here is of a different kind than any help in the world. Transcendent help reveals itself to him solely in the fact that he can be himself. That he can stand by himself, he owes to an intangible hand, extended to him from transcendence, a hand whose presence he can feel only in his freedom.

Man as object of investigation and man as freedom are known to us from radically different sources. The former is a content of knowledge, the latter a fundamental trait of our faith. But if freedom for its part becomes a content of knowledge and an object of investigation, a special form of superstition arises:

Faith stands on the road to freedom that is not an absolute and not an empty freedom, but that is experienced as the possibility of being given or not given to oneself. It is only through freedom that I become certain of transcendence. By freedom, to be sure, I attain to a point of independence from the world, but precisely through the consciousness of my radical attachment to transcendence. For it is not through myself that I am.

Superstition on the other hand arises by way of a something that is the express content of faith, and thus also through a supposed knowledge of freedom. A modern form of superstition for example is psycho-analysis taken as a philosophy, and the pseudo-medicine that makes man's freedom a supposed object of scientific research.

As I conceive of the nature of my humanity, so I conceive of transcendence—i.e. I conceive of it either as something that limits me or as something that enables me to soar, it is superstition steeped in the object (hence associated with scientific aberration), or faith, inner experience of the Comprehensive (hence associated with the consummation of non-knowledge).

Man, in common with everything he sees around him, in common with the beasts, is branded as a finite creature. But his human finiteness *cannot become self-contained*, in the same sense as the animal.

Every animal is perfect in its own way, in its limitation it fulfils itself within a continually repeated life cycle. It is exposed only to the natural process in which all things merge and are brought forth. Only man cannot fulfil himself in his finiteness. It is only man whose finiteness involves him in history, in which he strives to realize his potentialities. His openness is a sign of his freedom.

Because man cannot fulfil himself in his finite existence, because he must for ever search and strive (rather
than live unconsciously in the unchanging rut of recurrent cycles), he, alone of all living creatures, knows
that he is finite. Because of his incapacity for perfection,
his finiteness becomes more to him than is revealed in
the mere knowledge of the end. Man feels lost in it,
and as a result becomes aware of his task and potentialities. He finds himself in the most desperate situation,
but in such a way, that from it issues the strongest
appeal to raise himself up through his freedom. And
that is why man has again and again been represented
as the most astoundingly contradictory of creatures, the
most wretched and the most magnificent.

The proposition that man is finite and unfulfillable
has an ambivalent character. It is an insight, it derives
from demonstrable knowledge of the finite. But in its
universality it points to a faith content, in which the
freedom of human tasks is generated. In the fundamental experience of his nature, transcending the plane
of knowledge, he is aware of both his unfulfilment and
his infinite potentiality, his bondage and his freedom
that breaks through this bondage.

Conscious of his freedom, man desires to become
what he can and should be. He conceives an *ideal* of
his nature. As on the plane of cognition, the idea of
man as an object of scientific inquiry may lead to a
falsely definitive image of him, so on the plane of freedom he may falsely choose a path leading to an absolute

ideal. From helpless questioning and bewilderment, he thus aspires to take refuge in a universal that he can imitate in its concrete forms.

There are numerous images of man that have served as ideals with which we wished to identify ourselves. There is no doubt that such ideals have been effective, and that social types actually influence our behaviour. The ideal can be magnified to a vague conception of man's 'greatness', of something in man that is in a sense more than human, that is superhuman or inhuman.

For our philosophical consciousness it is crucial that we convince ourselves of the untruth and impossibility of such paths. Kant has given us the purest expression of this.[1] 'To attempt to realize the ideal in an example, that is, as a real phenomenon, as we might represent a perfectly wise man in a novel, is impossible, nay, absurd, and but little encouraging, because the natural limits, which are constantly interfering with the perfection in the idea, make all illusion in such an experiment impossible, and thus render the good itself in the idea suspicious and unreal.'

Just as we lose sight of man when he becomes an object of scientific inquiry in racial theory, psychoanalysis, or Marxism, and is represented as fully understandable, so we lose sight of the human task when he becomes an ideal.

The ideal is something fundamentally different from the idea. There is no ideal of man, but there is an idea

[1] *Critique of Pure Reason*, tr. by F. Max Müller (New York 1927), p. 461.

of man. Ideals of man collapse, the idea of man serves as a goal to his march forward. Ideals can in a sense be schemata of ideas, road signs. That is the truth in the great philosophical conceptions of the Noble Man in China, or of the Stoic Wise Man. They are not images of fulfilment, they only stimulate man's desire to rise above himself.

Something else again is orientation by the honoured and beloved historical figure. We may ask: What would he say in this case, how would he act? And we enter into a living discussion with him, though without regarding him as the absolutely true model to be imitated unconditionally. For each man is a man, and therefore lives in finiteness and imperfection, and also in error.

All ideals of man are impossible, because man's potentialities are infinite. There can be no perfect man. This has important philosophical consequences.

(1) The true value of man lies not in the species or type that he approximates, but in the historical individual, for whom no substitution or replacement is possible. The value of each individual man can be regarded as unassailable only when men cease to be regarded as expendable material, to be stamped by a universal. The social and professional types that we approximate have bearing only on our role in the world.

(2) The idea that all men are equal is obviously false, in so far as psychological aptitudes and talents are concerned—it is also untrue considered as the reality of a

social order, in which at best there can be equal opportunities and equity before the law.

The essential equality of all men lies alone in those depths, where to each man the road is opened by freedom to attain to God by leading an ethical life. It is the equality of a value that no human knowledge can ascertain or objectify, of the individual as an eternal soul. It is the equality of rights, and of the eternal judgment according to which a man merits a place in heaven or hell. This equality means: a respect for every man which forbids that any man should be treated only as a means and not at the same time as an end in himself.

The danger facing man is the self-assurance which tells him that he already is what he is capable of becoming. The faith by which he finds the road of his potentialities becomes then a possession that concludes his road, whether it take the form of moral self-complacency or of pride in his innate gifts.

From the Stoic view that man should live so as to be pleasing to himself, to the harmony with himself that Kant ascribes to the man who acts in an ethical way, there has prevailed an arbitrary self-complacency, to which St. Paul and St. Augustine, indeed Kant himself, opposed the idea of man corrupted in the root.

The essential is that man as existence in his freedom should experience the fact of being given to himself by transcendence. Then human freedom is at the heart of all his potentialities and through transcendence, through the one, man is guided to his own inner unity.

This *guidance* is radically different from any guidance

in the world; for it offers no objective certainty; it coincides with man's complete attainment of freedom. For it operates only by way of the freedom of subjective certainty. God's voice resides in the light that comes as his own conviction to the individual open to tradition and his environment. God's voice becomes audible in the freedom of subjective conviction, and this is the only organ by which it can impart itself to man. Where man's resolve arises out of his depths, he believes that he is obeying God, though he has no objective guaranty for his knowledge of God's will.

Guidance operates through man's judgment concerning his own acts. This judgment checks him and spurs him on, corrects and confirms. But in fact, man can never wholly and definitively base his judgment concerning himself upon himself. He desires to hear the judgment of his fellow men, in order to attain clarity through communication. But the crucial judgment is not in the last analysis that of the people he esteems, although this is the only judgment that is accessible to him in practice. The decisive judgment would be that of God.

Thus in time the truth of judgment is ultimately attained only by way of subjective conviction, whether the moral law claims universal or only historical validity.

Inward obedience to the freely accepted, universal ethical law—to the ten commandments—is bound up with the realization that transcendence is present in this very freedom.

But since specific action cannot logically be deduced

from the universal law, God's guiding voice can be heard more directly in the primal source of the historically concrete law than in the universal. But for all the subjective certainty this voice gives, its meaning remains uncertain. Obedience to God's voice always involves the risk of error. For its message is susceptible of many interpretations, the freedom that would consist in the clear and unmistakable knowledge of the necessary is never complete. The risk implied in the question of whether in this matter I am really myself, whether I have truly heard the guiding voice from the primal spring of being, never ceases.

In time, this consciousness of risk remains the condition for increasing freedom. It excludes complete reliance on subjective certainty, forbids the generalization of the subjective commandment into a universal law, and bars fanaticism. Even in the certainty of the resolve, there must, in so far as it is translated into practical action, remain a certain margin of indetermination. There can be no subjective security. The pride of the absolute truth destroys truth in the world. The humility of the permanent question is inherent in subjective certainty. For it is always possible that things will subsequently look quite different. Even the clear, but never adequately clear, conscience can embark on error.

Only in retrospect are we justified in admiring the unfathomable wisdom of God's guidance. But even then it is never certain, God's unfathomable guidance can never become a possession.

From the psychological point of view, God's voice has no other expression in time than man's judgment of himself. This judgment may come upon man with a sudden certainty, after man has honestly and carefully striven for it, weighing all the contradictory possibilities; and then he discovers in it God's judgment, though it is never definitive and always equivocal. But only in exalted moments is it audible. It is by such moments and for such moments that we live.

The road of the thinking man is a philosophical life. Philosophizing is a specifically human pursuit. Man is the only being in the world to whom being is manifested through his empirical existence. He cannot fulfil himself in empirical existence as such, he cannot content himself with the enjoyment of empirical existence. He breaks through all the empirical realities that find their seeming fulfilment in the world. As a man he only attains to real knowledge of himself when, open to being as a whole, he relates his life in the world to transcendence. In the very effort to master his empirical existence, he strives toward being. For he cannot adequately account for his sojourn in the world by the laws immanent to the world. Accordingly, he goes beyond his empirical existence, beyond the world, to the ground of existence and the world, where he attains awareness of his primal source. Here, though in a sense he is in communion with creation, he does not find a secure refuge, nor is he at his goal. He must seek eternity in his life, which mediates between the primal source and the goal.

In unfaith the human condition becomes a biological fact among other biological facts; man surrenders to what his finite knowledge determines as necessities and inevitabilities, he gives in to a sense of futility, the energy of his mind declines. He stifles in his supposed factuality.

Philosophical faith, on the other hand, is the faith of man in his potentialities. In it breathes his freedom.

Chapter Four

PHILOSOPHY AND RELIGION

THROUGHOUT THE MILLENNIA philosophy and
religion have stood in alliance with, or in
hostility to one another.

They go hand in hand, originally in the myths and
cosmologies, later in theology—for philosophy has
appeared in the cloak of theology, just as at other times
it has worn the dress of poetry and, most frequently,
of science.

But, then, as the two separate, religion becomes for
philosophy the great mystery that it cannot understand.
The cult, the claim to revelation, the claim to power of
a community founded on religion, of its organization
and politics, and the interpretation that religion confers
upon itself, become objects of philosophical inquiry.

In this attitude of inquiry lies the germ of the
struggle. For philosophy, the struggle can only take
the form of a striving for truth by exclusively intellectual means.

Neither religion nor philosophy is a clearly defined
entity; we cannot take them as fixed points from which
to start on our comparative investigation. They are

both involved in historical transformation, but both conceive of themselves at all times as vehicles of eternal truth, whose historical garb at once conceals and transmits the truth. I cannot speak of the one eternal religious truth. Philosophical truth is the *philosophia perennis* to which no one can lay claim, but with which everyone engaged in philosophical thought is concerned, and which is present wherever there are true philosophers.

There is no standpoint outside the opposition of philosophy and religion. Each one of us stands at one of the poles and speaks of some crucial aspect of the other, without personal experience. Consequently you can expect me too to be blind in certain points and to misunderstand. I hesitate and yet I must speak. To speak of religion, without being personally involved in it, is questionable, but it is indispensable as a means of expressing one's own clear deficiency, as a means of seeking after the truth, and also of testing religious faith by the questions that thus arise. Religion is no enemy of philosophy, but something that essentially concerns it and troubles it.

But to-day we are in a situation that I shall illustrate by a personal reference. Because religion is of such prime importance, awareness of my deficiency made me eager to hear what was being said in religious circles. It is among the sorrows of my life, spent in the search for truth, that discussion with theologians always dries up at crucial points; they fall silent, state an incomprehensible proposition, speak of something else, make some categoric statement, engage in amiable talk, without really taking cognizance of what one has said—and in the last analysis they are not really interested. For on the one hand they are certain of their truth, terrifyingly certain; and on the other hand they do not regard it as worth while to bother about people like us, who strike them as merely stubborn. And communication requires listening and real answers, forbids silence or the evasion of questions; it demands above all that all statements of faith (which are after all made in human language and directed toward objects, and which constitute an attempt to get one's bearings in the world) should continue to be questioned and tested, not only outwardly, but inwardly as well. No one who is in definitive possession of the truth, can speak properly with someone else—he breaks off authentic communication in favour of the belief he holds.

I can touch on this great problem only from certain angles and only inadequately. I am concerned in this discussion with throwing light on the original philosophical faith.

Religion, contrasted with philosophy, reveals the following characteristics:

Religion has its cult, is bound up with a peculiar community of men, arising from the cult, and it is inseparable from the myth. Religion always embodies man's practical relation to the transcendent, in the shape of something holy in the world, as delimited from the profane or unholy. Where this is no longer present, or is rejected, the peculiar character of religion has vanished. Almost the whole of mankind, as far as historical memory extends, has lived religiously, and this is an indication that can scarcely be ignored, of the truth and central importance of religion.

Philosophy proper, on the other hand, knows no cult, no community led by a priesthood, no existent invested with a sacred character and set apart from other existents in the world. What religion localizes in a specific place, can for philosophy be present everywhere and always. Philosophy is a product of the individual's freedom, not of socially determined conditions, and it does not carry the sanction of a collectivity. Philosophy has no rites, no roots in a primitive mythology. Men take it from a free tradition and transform it as they make it their own. Although pertaining to man as man, it remains the concern of individuals.

Religion is intent upon embodying its truth in tangible symbols, philosophy pursues only effective subjective certainty.—To religion the God of the philosophers seems threadbare, pale, empty; it disparagingly calls the philosophical state of mind 'deism'; to philosophy the tangible symbols of religion seem like deceptive veils and misleading simplifications.—Religion denounces the God of philosophy as a mere abstraction, philosophy distrusts the religious images of God as seductive idols, magnificent as they may be.

Yet, though the manifestations of philosophy and religion seem to clash, there is a contact, and even a convergence in their contents, as may be illustrated by the ideas of God, prayer, revelation.

The idea of God: In the West, the idea of the one God arose in Greek philosophy and in the Old Testament. In both cases, a stupendous work of abstraction was effected, but in entirely different ways.

In Greek philosophy monotheism arose as an idea, it was postulated from ethical considerations, it imposed itself on the mind in an atmosphere of philosophic serenity. It did not set its imprint upon masses of men, but upon individuals. Its results were individuals of a high human type and a free philosophy. It was not an effective civilizing agent.

In the Old Testament, on the other hand, monotheism grew up in the passion of battle for the pure, the true, the one God. The abstraction was not accomplished by logic but by a reaction against the images and embodiments of the deity, which veil God more than they reveal him, and a revolt against the seductions of the cult, against Dionysian rites, and against belief in the efficacy of sacrifice. This cult of the one, living God was won in battle against the Baals, against immanent religion with its shallow optimism, its festivals and orgies, its self-complacency and moral indifference.

This true God suffers no image and likeness, sets no store by cult and sacrifice, by temple and rites and laws, but only by righteous actions and love of our fellow men (Micah, Isaiah, Jeremiah).—The monotheistic abstraction, like nihilism, negates all worldly existence, but actually springs from the spiritual fullness of a mind to which the supra-mundane creator-God with his ethical laws has revealed himself.—This abstraction is not based upon the development of an idea, but upon the word of God, upon God himself, who was experienced in the word which the prophet imparted as the word of God. The force of God's reality refracted in such a prophetic mind, and not the power of an idea, brought forth this monotheism. Hence the miraculous part of it is that in thought content the monotheism of the Greeks and of the Old Testament should coincide, though they differ radically as to the mode of God's presence. The difference is that between philosophy and religion. Consequently it is also the difference between divinity and God—between transcendence as an intellectual idea, and the living God; the One of philosophy is not the One of the Bible.

But if philosophical clarity prevails, the question arises whether the incomparable faith of the prophets, that moves us so deeply even to-day, was possible only because they were still intellectually naïve, still unaffected by philosophical thought, and accordingly failed to notice that the 'word', spoken immediately by God, still embodied a remnant of sensible reality—of the image and likeness which they combated.

Greek and Old Testament monotheism have together dominated the Western idea of God. They interpreted each other. That was possible because the faith of the prophets effected an abstraction that is analogous to philosophical abstraction. The prophetic faith is more powerful than the philosophical idea, because it arises from the direct experience of God. But in intellectual clarity it is inferior to philosophy;

hence it was lost in the subsequent religious development, even in the Bible.

Prayer: The cult is the act of the community, prayer is an act of the individual in his solitude. The cult exists everywhere, while prayer is discernible here and there in history; in the Bible it becomes distinct only with Jeremiah. The liturgy, in which the cult is embodied, contains a number of texts that are called prayers, because they serve to invoke, praise, and supplicate the godhead. But their salient feature is that they originated in the remotest past, that although they once grew and changed over a period of generations, they have since then retained rigid, immutable forms and are experienced as something permanent. Parts of them have long since become incomprehensible, they either play the role of a mystery or have been endowed with a new, transformed meaning. In contradistinction to this, prayer is individual, existentially present. As a subordinate element of the cult, it is performed by the individual in a fixed form, and then he remains entirely within the sphere of religion. But when it is really personal and primal, prayer stands at the frontier of philosophy, and it becomes philosophy in the moment when it is divested of any pragmatic relation to the godhead or desire to influence the godhead for practical ends. It marks a break with the concreteness of a personal relation to a personal God, which is one of the sources of religion, and a movement toward abstract philosophical contemplation; at first it expresses only devotion and gratitude to God, but later it becomes progressively internalized and man finds in it a firm ground on which to stand. The aim of this contemplation is no longer to achieve practical mundane results, but inward transfiguration. Where such speculative spiritualization developed into genuine contemplation, it was like one continuous prayer. While this contemplation was a part of the whole that is embodied in religion, to-day it has become separate from religious activity and possible by itself.

Revelation: Religions are based on revelation; this is clearly and consciously the case with the Indian and Biblical religions. Revelation is the immediate utterance of God, localized in time and valid for all men, through word, commandment, action, event. God issues his commandments, he institutes the congregation, founds the cult. Thus the cult of the Christians is founded as an act of God, who instituted the Lord's Supper. Since the content of a religion derives originally from revelation, this content is not valid in itself, but only within a community—the people, the congregation, the church—which is its actual authority and guaranty.

With reference to the efforts to arrive at a philosophical concept of God, these efforts in which each step seems to cancel out the preceding—we often hear it said that any attempt to arrive at God by thought is vain, and that man knows God and can know God only through revelation. God gave the law, God sent the prophets, He himself descended in the form of his servant, to redeem us on the Cross.

But revelation that is communicated as such, must

have a mundane form. Once it is stated, it deteriorates into finiteness, and even into trivial rationality. In speech, its meaning is perverted. The word of man is not the word of God. That part of revelation that concerns man as man, becomes a content of philosophy and as such is valid without revelation. Have we to do with attenuation of religion, a loss of its substance?—then we call the process secularization. Or have we to do with a purification, a deepening, a distillation or even realization of its primal essence? Both processes would seem to exist. The danger of an emptying by rationalization is coupled with the possibility that man may realize an authentic truth.

Since antiquity religion has been continually rejected by philosophers. Here let us list a number of typical objections to religion and attempt to examine each one critically and assign to it its proper place.

(a) 'The existence of so many religions proves that none is true. For there is only one truth.'

This argument stands only if statements of faith are assimilated to contents of knowledge; it does not apply to religious faith itself. Religious faith has its historical manifestation; its outward expression must not be confused with the inner meaning of religious life itself, which speaks in it: *Una religio in rituum varietate* (Nicholas of Cusa).

(b) 'Up to the present time religions have sanctioned every evil, they have perpetrated or justified the most atrocious deeds, violence, lies, human sacrifice, the crusades, the religious wars.'

It is hard to draw up a balance sheet of good and evil in the workings of religion. Every value judgment must be based on an investigation of the historical facts. The reproach must be considered along with the salutary effects of religion in deepening the soul, in ordering human affairs, in its vast welfare activities, in supplying meaningful themes to art and thought.

But if one should go so far as to argue that good relations among men, peace and order, are more readily realized through reason than through religion; that justice is more efficacious than faith, practical morality than religious belief; that what is good in mankind is the work of science and reason, not of religion—then it must be answered that religion does not exclude reason, and that up to now religion has in fact realized the most enduring and most meaningful order, with the help of reason, not by direct injunctions but through the devotion and responsibility of believing men. While thus far all attempts to build solely on reason—and here the understanding is meant—have been speedily followed by nihilistic chaos.

(c) 'Religion evokes false fears. Illusions torment the soul. The torments of hell, the wrath of God, the incomprehensible reality of a merciless will, etc. are sources of horror, particularly on the deathbed. The liberation from religion brings peace of mind, because it is a liberation from delusions.'

This argument is sound, in so far as specific superstitions are meant. It is false when it is applied to the fear itself. If innumerable souls have been impelled to

choose good instead of evil by the fear of hell, it is only
seldom that such fear is nothing other than fear of a
supposed reality. Often the figuration of hell serves to
translate profound existential motives for the choice,
motives within one's own being. Existential anguish
is a basic characteristic of the awakened man. The peace
of mind that arises from the negation of hell does not
suffice; it must be rooted in a positive confidence, a
basic attitude of the soul, which follows the good will
which continually overcomes fear. Where there is no
fear, man is superficial.

(d) 'The religions foster an all-pervading disregard
of truth. Because they put the unfathomed, the thoughtless, the absurd at the beginning and withdraw it from
all questioning, they create a dominant mood of dull
obedience. Wherever a question arises, the religious
man does violence to his own intelligence, and looks
on this lack of integrity as a virtue. The habit of not
questioning makes for untruthfulness in other spheres.
The religious man overlooks the contradictions in his
own thinking and behaviour. He permits perversions
of what was originally true, because he fails to notice
them. There is an affinity between religious faith and
contempt of truth.'

In answer to this argument we can only say that the
same phenomena do not necessarily occur in the original
religions as in their later developments. Even if, according to Jakob Burckhardt, the degree in which the
religious artists were lacking in critical sense can
scarcely be understood by modern man, the lack of

critical sense does not necessarily imply disregard of truth. Limits and mysteries that the understanding tends to conceal from itself, are directly present in the religious mind, though in a mythical form with a tendency to degenerate into superstition.

(e) 'Religions define as sacred, things which are indeed profane and made solely by men. The halo of mystery which they cast about these things tends to devaluate everything else in the world. Where an attitude of reverence is bound to religion, it tends to induce irreverence in all spheres to which religion does not penetrate. The attitude of reverence with regard to all manifestations of being is lost, if reverence is specifically localized. Such delimitation implies both exclusion and destruction.'

This reproach by no means applies to all religious men. Religion is, on the contrary, capable of bringing the whole world into its light, of casting a reflection of its specific radiance upon all realities. But the argument does apply to many realizations of religion, even though such realizations will perhaps be condemned by the religious man himself as distortions.

None of these discussions of religion touches upon what is crucial. These anti-religious arguments strike the distorted versions of the various religions, not religion itself.

Moreover, we have spoken only of religion and religions, not of what represents and proclaims itself as a unique revealed truth and declines to be classified as one religion among many. This is the case in the churches and denominations deriving from the comprehensive Biblical religion to which all of us belong, Jews and Christians, Greek Orthodox, Catholics and Protestants, and perhaps Mohammedans as well.

In this connection there are two propositions (one negative and one positive) that result from philosophical faith. I should like to explain them here:

(1) The claim to exclusivity was an original element in Biblical religion and this claim has been manifested in all its ramifications, but perhaps it is not necessary to Biblical religion, and perhaps it will not be raised for ever. Both in its motive and in its consequences, this claim is catastrophic for men. We must fight for the truth and for our soul against this fatal claim.

(2) Biblical religion is one of the wellsprings of our philosophy, and in it we gather irreplaceable truth.

We regard both propositions as important. They are bound up with a question that has a bearing on the entire destinies of the West: what is the future of Biblical religion?

Against the claim to exclusivity.

The substance of faith is regarded not merely as absolute truth, but also as exclusive truth. The Christian does not say: this is my way, but, this is *the* way; and he quotes Christ, the son of God, as saying: I am the way, the truth, and the life. The believer in Christ is permitted to think of himself: Ye are the salt of the earth: ye are the light of the world.

Such objections as the following may be raised: If God can have men as children, it seems more likely that all men, and not just a few, or certain individuals, should be his children.—The claim that only those who believe in Christ will have eternal life, is not convincing. For noble men and pure in soul are quite discernible outside of Christianity; it would be absurd for them to be lost, particularly if we compare them to certain among the most conspicuous Christians in history, who have been none too lovable or admirable in any human sense.—The inner conversion of man from his own self-will to boundless self-sacrifice and devotion is not found solely among Christians.—But all these arguments fail to strike the core.

Wherever in the world men are struck by a religious truth, this truth has absolute validity for them. Yet—outside the Biblical world—they do not thereby exclude the possibility of another truth for other men. From a philosophical point of view, this general attitude of men is also the sound one. And here we must clarify certain fundamental differences in the meaning of truth (which we had in mind in our discussion of Bruno and Galileo).

When I act absolutely because I believe absolutely, there is no sufficient reason and no goal on the basis of which my action is purposeful, that is, rationally intelligible. The absolute is not universal, but is historical in the impenetrable, self-illumined dynamism of the present act. It is profoundly unknown, much as can be known and said through it. Nothing can take its place, it is always unique and yet it may serve others not only as an orientation, but as a prototype by which to recognize something of their own, which differs from it in its historical manifestation and yet coincides with it in the light of eternity. That which is historically, existentially true is indeed absolute, but this does not mean that the expression or manifestation of it is a truth for all.

Conversely: what is universally valid for all (like scientific and other logically true propositions), is for that very reason not absolute, is universally valid for all from a specific standpoint and on the basis of a definite method, hence under certain conditions and not absolutely. This kind of true proposition is cogent for all whose intelligence can grasp it. But it is relative to the standpoint and method by which it is disclosed. It is existentially indifferent, because it is finite, particular, objectively cogent—no man can or should die for it.

In short: The absoluteness of historical truth implies the relativity of every formulation of it, and of all its historically finite manifestations. Universally valid statements can be based only upon relative standpoints and methods. Formulable faith contents must not be treated like universally true propositions; the absolute awareness of truth in faith is something fundamentally different from the comprehension of the universal validity of scientifically true propositions, which are always particular. Historical absoluteness does not carry with it the universal validity of its manifestations in word, dogma, cult, ritual, institutions. It is the confusion of the two that makes it possible to claim exclusivity for a religious truth.

It is in itself a fallacy to treat the universally valid in scientific knowledge as an absolute by which one might live, to expect of science what it can never achieve. True, my devotion to truth forbids me to overlook anything that is intellectually cogent, and enjoins me on the contrary to allow it full scope. But to claim for its content what only metaphysical meanings can provide, that is, a sense of contentment with being, of repose in being, is a deception that offers not fulfilment but ultimate emptiness.

But the opposite fallacy is really fatal: to transform the absoluteness of existential decision into a knowledge of truth that can be stated in the form of moral law, or to pervert the historical absoluteness of faith into a universal truth for all.

The consequence of such fallacies is self-deception concerning what I really am and desire, it is intolerance (refusal to countenance anything but my own statements that have solidified into dogmas) and incapacity for communication (inability to hear anyone else or to admit honest questioning of oneself). Impulses such as the will to power, cruelty, the impulse to destroy, become ultimately the real motive forces behind the mask of this perverted will to truth. And then these impulses, finding a hideously false justification in their ostensible advocacy of truth, move toward their more or less open satisfaction.

Only in the sphere of Biblical religion does this exclusivity of the apprehended truth of faith appear to belong to the faith itself, to be consciously professed and developed in all its consequences. For the believer this can be a new supernatural mark for the truth of his faith. Philosophical insight, on the other hand, sees not only the untruth implied in the fundamental *quid pro quo* of such faith, but also the terrible consequences.

We may take as an example of this Biblical religion, Christianity with its claim to absolute truth for all. Our knowledge of the extraordinary accomplishments of Christianity, of the noble figures who have lived in this faith and by this faith cannot prevent us from seeing how this fundamental perversion brought forth historical evils that wore the cloak of sacred and absolute truth.

Let us consider some of the consequences of this claim to exclusivity. Even the New Testament makes Jesus, who turns the other cheek and preaches the Sermon on the Mount, utter the words: I bring not peace but a sword. He presents the alternative to follow him or not to follow him: he who is not with me is against me.

And innumerable Christian believers in history have acted in keeping with this injunction. According to their doctrine of salvation, all those men are lost who lived before Christ or without Christ. The many religions are a sum of untruths or at best of partial truths; their adherents are all heathen. They are summoned to give up their religion and follow the faith of Christ. The universal mission not only proclaimed the faith to all peoples with all the instruments of propaganda, but it has continually revealed an underlying will to force belief where it was not accepted voluntarily (*coge intrare*). Campaigns of annihilation, crusades were unleashed. The Christian denominations even carried on religious wars among themselves. Politics became a weapon of the churches.

Thus the will to power became a basic factor in this religion, which originally had nothing to do with power. The claim to world domination is a consequence of the claim to exclusive truth. In the great process of secularization—that is, the movement to retain Biblical values while casting off their religious form—even the fanaticism of unbelief shows the influence of its Biblical origin. The secularized philosophical positions within the Western civilizations have frequently revealed this trait of absolutism, this persecution of other beliefs, this aggressive profession of faith, this inquisitorial attitude towards other faiths, always in consequence of absolute claims to a truth which each one believes he possesses.

In view of all this, philosophical faith must reluctantly recognize that where discussion is broken off and reason countenanced only under certain conditions, the best intentions of maintaining open communication are doomed to failure.

I do not understand how any one can maintain an attitude of neutrality toward the claim to exclusivity. That would be possible if intolerance could be regarded as a strange and harmless anomaly. But this is by no means the case with the claim to exclusivity that is rooted in the Bible. By its very nature it tends to assert itself through powerful institutions that keep constantly arising, and it stands for ever in readiness to kindle new fires in which to burn heretics. This lies in the very nature of the claim to exclusivity in all forms of the Biblical religion, regardless of how many believers have personally not the slightest leaning toward violence, let alone toward the annihilation of those whom they regard as unbelievers.

Because intolerance against intolerance (but only against intolerance) is indispensable, intolerance against the exclusivist claim is necessary when it not only propounds a doctrine for consideration by others, but strives to force it on others by law, by compulsory schools, etc.

Quite different is the Christian faith that frees itself from the exclusivist claim and its consequences. Our era confronts us with the question whether the declining belief in Christ—which would by no means mean the end of Christianity as a Biblical religion—is only a temporary decline or whether it is the consequence of a definitive historical transformation. To-day it appears that fewer and fewer people believe in Christ as the only begotten son of God, as the unique mediator sent by God. The truth of this is hard to test. Men of high personal stature still seem to be imbued with faith. No one can say in advance whether a transformed faith in Christ can be captured and made into the motive force of a Biblical religion freed from the stigma of exclusivity. And what this faith would mean, is a question to be decided within the framework of the Biblical religion

after it has succeeded by virtue of its own profound
dynamism in reintegrating this absolutized form of it,
which is abjuring its true origin.

The claim to exclusivity is present in the Christian
faith, in the Jewish doctrine of the law, in the various
forms of national religion, in Islam. Biblical religion is
the inclusive historical area from which, if we overlook
other contents, each denomination derives its particular
emphasis. The whole Bible, including the Old and the
New Testament, is the sacred book only of the Christian denominations. For the Jews the New Testament,
which was produced by Jews, is not regarded as part of
the Bible; but in its ethical and monotheistic content it
is no less important for the Jewish religion than for the
Christian. Islam does not regard the Bible as sacred,
although Islam sprang from the same religious foundation under the influence of Jews and Christians.

The Bible and Biblical religion have from a philosophical point of view this essential characteristic: they
form no total doctrine and offer nothing definitive.
The claim to exclusivity does not belong to Biblical
religion as a whole, but only to certain forms that mark
fixations of the historical movement of this religion.
The claim to exclusivity is the work of man and not
built on God, who provided man with many roads to
himself.

The Bible and Biblical religion are a foundation of
our philosophy, a lasting orientation and a source of
irreplaceable contents. Western philosophy—whether
we admit it or not—is always with the Bible, even when

it combats it. In concluding the present lecture, we should like to make certain remarks concerning the positive contributions of the Bible to philosophy.

For the Biblical religion.

In the Bible the most extreme rationally inevitable contradictions come to expression.

(1) From the sacrifice of the patriarchs to the complicated daily sacrificial service in the temple at Jerusalem and the Lord's Supper of the Christians, the cultic religion runs through the Bible. Within this cultic religion a tendency to limit and spiritualize the cult continually makes its appearance—as in the elimination of the 'high places' (the many sites of the cult throughout the country) in favour of the one cult in the temple at Jerusalem—similarly in the transformation of the locally experienced and living cult into an official, abstract ritual—and also in the sublimation of the cult from the sacrificial service to the Lord's Supper and the Mass. Cult it always remains. But the prophets begin to turn passionately against the cult itself (not only against the false interpretation of the cult). Yahweh says (Amos v. 21): 'I hate, I despise your feast days, and I will not dwell in your solemn assemblies. Though ye offer me burnt offerings and your meat offerings, I will not accept them: neither will I regard the peace offerings of your fat beasts. Take thou away from me the noise of thy songs; for I will not hear the melody of thy viols.' And again Yahweh speaks (Hosea vi. 6): 'For I desired mercy, and not sacrifice; and the knowledge of God more than burnt offerings.'

(2) From the decalogue and the covenant to the compendious laws of Deuteronomy and Leviticus, runs the development of the religion of the law. The law is present in the revelation of God through the word of the Torah; it is written. But Jeremiah turns against the written law as such: 'The pen of the scribes hath made it into lies' (Jeremiah vii. 8). God's law does not reside in the fixed law of Scripture, but in the heart: 'After those days, saith the Lord, I will put their laws in their inward parts, and write it in their hearts' (xxxi. 33).

(3) Beginning with the conclusion of the covenant in the days of Moses, the Jews' consciousness of being *the chosen people* runs through the Bible. But at a very early time the chosenness is also suspended. 'Are ye not as children of the Ethiopians unto me, O children of Israel?' says Yahweh. 'Have not I brought up Israel out of the land of Egypt and the Philistines from Caphtor, and the Syrians from Kir?' (Amos ix. 7). Here the peoples enjoy equal rank. In the period of exile, God becomes once more the God of Israel—but at the same time in His role of creator, He becomes the universal God, who lives for all peoples and even takes pity on the heathen of Nineveh as against the small-hearted Jonah.

(4) Jesus becomes the Christ God. But contrary to this from the outset are the words of Jesus himself: 'Why callest thou me good? there is none good but one, that is, God.' (Mark x. 18.)

Such examples can be multiplied. One might venture the assertion that in the Bible seen as a whole, every-

G
97

thing occurs in polarities. For every formulation one will ultimately find the opposite formulation. Nowhere is the whole, full, pure truth—because it cannot exist in any sentence of human speech or in any living human figure. In our limited view of things, we are always losing sight of the other pole. We touch upon the truth only when, in clear consciousness of the polarities, we approach it through them.

Thus we find opposed to one another: the religion of the cult and the prophetic religion of the pure ethos; the religion of the law and the religion of love; the locking of religion into rigid forms (in order to preserve the precious heritage of faith down through the generations) and its opening up for the man who only believes in God and loves him; the religion of the priests and the free religion of prayer that is carried on by individuals; the national God and the universal God; the covenant with the chosen people and the covenant with man as man; the balancing of guilt and retribution in this life (happiness and unhappiness considered as measures of virtue and sin) and the attitude of faith of Jeremiah, of Job in the presence of the divine mystery; the religion of the congregation and the religion of the men of God, seers, prophets; magical religion and the ethical religion of the rational idea of creation. The Bible indeed embraces the great antitheses of faith: the anti-faith of demonology, of deification of men, of nihilism (this last in Ecclesiastes). The consequence of these polarities within the Bible is that in subsequent history all parties and trends have been able to invoke some passage in the Bible. The polarities that are clearly developed in the Bible have recurred over and over again, Jewish theocracy in Christian churches, the freedom of the prophets in the mystics and reformers, the chosen people in any number of Christian peoples, communities, sects which have regarded themselves as chosen. The Biblical religion has repeatedly inspired returns to the original source, counteraction against fixations, living creative activity, as though it were the destiny of Western civilization, which is grounded in the sacred book, to find in their authority a prefiguration of all life's contradictions, and thus to be made free for all possibilities and for the unremitting struggle for the elevation of man, who knows that in his free activity he is given to himself by God.

The Bible embraces in its texts spiritual deposits of the most primitive and most sublime human realities. This it has in common with other great documents of religion.

But even the barbaric element in the beginning has that ancient grandeur which makes us hesitate to call it merely barbaric. There is in it a simplicity of expression, a naïve strength.

Through the Bible runs a passion that makes a unique impression, because it refers to God. God is in the fire of the volcano, in the earthquake, in the storm. He rises to inaccessible heights, lets the storms serve as His messengers, while He himself becomes mysteriously present in the still small voice—and as He rises above all images, He rises also above these sensible manifestations, to become the purely transcendent creator, the universal God, who is inconceivable, above all passions, impenetrable in His decisions, but always in a sense personal in the pathos by which man knows himself to be seized.

Because they stand before this God, the men of the Bible, even while they know themselves to be nothing, grow to superhuman stature. These men of God and prophets without weapons are spiritual heroes, who maintain themselves against the world around them— sometimes in single combat against all others—because they feel themselves to be servants of God. The legendary Moses and Elijah, the real figures of Amos, Isaiah, and Jeremiah, have indeed the stature of Michelangelo's vision.

The heroism of the Bible is not the defiance of force, standing upon itself. The impossible is ventured at the behest of God. The heroism is sublimated.

But the original idea of God that makes this possible can easily degenerate. Then heroism is denatured into the ugly, distorted stubbornness of a perverse spirit. A schizophrenic (Ezekiel) can—once—influence all history.

But there are also words in the Bible that seem quiet and pure as the truth itself. They are rare and they are immersed in a whirlwind of the most extreme possibilities. The immoderate, eccentric and ugly is an element in the Bible. And finally, a veil of sophism and monotony lies over the whole. But even here those energies must have been at work which prevented the religion of Ezra from taking on a deadly rigidity; the fire which gave rise to Job, the Psalms, Ruth and Ecclesiastes, was preserved.

The permanent bond between the truth of the Bible and the substance of myths, sociological realities, untenable cosmologies, primitive, pre-scientific knowledge, caused the phenomenon of Biblical truth, which in itself is living history, to become subsequently a mere thing of the past. Even in the Bible the garments of this truth are interchangeable.

Except for a very few rudiments, the Bible is lacking in philosophical self-consciousness. Hence the power of the speaking existence, the source of revealed truth —but hence also the persistent excesses in opposite directions. The guidance of critical thought is lacking. Passion is corrected by passion.

The Bible is the deposit of a thousand years of human borderline experience. Through these experiences the mind of man was illumined, he achieved certainty of God and thus of himself. And this is what creates the unique atmosphere of the Bible.

In the Bible we see man in his fundamental modes of failure. But in such a way that existential experience, and realization, are manifested precisely in his failure.

In our approach to the Bible the essential is always to regain from the deviations the truth that is always the same, though it is never objectively, definitively present. True transformation is a return to the primal source. Garments that have grown old must be cast off, garments suited to the present must be found. But the primal source is not what was in the beginning, but what is eternally present and authentic. On the other hand, to formulate the primal truth is to dress it in a temporal garment. Yet in time, this garment corresponds to the temporal form of faith.

But it is not only old clothes that must be cast off; the primal source must also be retrieved from its fixations and perversions—the polar tensions must be re-established—one must strive, always in the simplest possible way, to clarify and enhance the eternal truth.

(1) *The retrieving of the truth from fixations:* The truth of Biblical religion runs counter to the fixations that have been effected within it, that were once perhaps historically valid, but are no longer valid for philosophical reflection. If I am not mistaken, examples of such fixations are the national religion, the religion of the law, the specific religion of Christ:

We must abandon the idea of a national religion. In the early stage of the Biblical religion, the Israelite cult of Yahweh actually was national. Protestant and especially Calvinistic tendencies revived religious nationalism when they based their Christianity more on parts of the Old Testament than on the whole of it and on the New Testament.

We must abandon the religion of the law, which took form in Ezra and Nehemiah, in the most important sections of Leviticus, and in the Talmud, and which assumed its specific form as Judaism, in the narrow sense of the term. Along with the religion of the law, we must abandon the rule of the priesthood (hierocracy), which was created and realized by the Jews under foreign domination, and which was continued or demanded by Christian churches.

We must abandon the religion of Christ, that sees God in Christ and bases the doctrine of salvation on an idea of sacrifice found in Deutero-Isaiah and applied to Christ.

Each of these three forms of religion becomes narrow, though they all originated in an element of truth. But the national religion as such cannot be the absolute religion and can only express a surface aspect of the truth. The religion of the law formalizes the profound idea of law, dissipates it in absurdities of all kinds.

The religion of Christ contains the truth that God speaks to man through man. But God speaks through many men, in the Bible through the successive pro-prophets of whom Jesus is the last. No man can be God; God speaks exclusively through no man, and what is more, His speech through every man has many meanings.

The religion of Christ furthermore embodies the truth of referring the individual to himself. The spirit of Christ belongs to every man. It is the *pneuma*, i.e. the spirit of an enthusiasm surging upward to the supra-sensory. It is also the openness to one's own suffering as a road to transcendence; he who has taken the cross upon himself can ascertain the authentic in failure. The spirit of Christ is finally a bond with the God-given *nobilitas ingenita* which I follow or which I betray, the actuality of the divine in man. But if the religion of Christ means that I should apprehend in faith the redeeming Christ outside me by realizing the spirit of Christ within me, then a twofold conclusion is inescapable for philosophical thought: the Christ within me is not exclusively bound up with the historical Jesus Christ; and Jesus as Christ, as the God-man, is a myth. The process of demythicization must not arbitrarily halt at this point. Even the profoundly meaningful myth remains a myth and a fancy, and becomes an objective guaranty only through a religious truth (that philosophy cannot see) or through deception.

(2) *The re-establishment of the polar tensions:* In order to appropriate the truth that is manifested in the Bible, we must be fully conscious of the contradictions that occur in it. Contradictions have diverse meanings. Rational contradictions lead to alternatives only one term of which can be formally true. Opposing forces always constitute a polar whole, through which the truth manifests itself. Dialectic contradictions constitute a movement of thought, through which the truth that is not accessible to direct statement speaks.

Biblical religion is distinguished by its abundance of contradiction, polar tension, dialectic. It is not by will alone, but by constant openness to the contradictory, that we can retain the dynamic energy of tension, or retrieve it where it has been lost. Rationalism and the desire for repose, as well as the destructive will to fight, strive to do away with the polarities, in order to establish the rule of the definitive and one-sided.

We can recognize in the Scriptures the fundamental tensions which up until now have kept the Western world in motion: God and the world, church and state, religion and philosophy, religion of the law and prophetic religion, cult and ethos.

The eternal truth can accordingly be apprehended only if we are open to the insoluble problems inherent in empirical existence, if we continuously question all our achievements, if we do not lose sight of extreme situations, of our absolute failures.

(3) *Clarification and enhancement of the eternal truth:* By our experience of the tensions, the dialectic and the contradictions striving toward a decision, we can positively apprehend what words can express only abstractly —the truth that we outlined in formulating the basic characteristics of Biblical religion. Let me restate the elements of this truth, which constitutes philosophical faith. They are:

the idea of the one God;

the realization of the absolute nature of the decision between good and evil in finite man;

love as the fundamental actualization of the eternal in man;

the act—both inward and external—as the test of man;

types of moral world order which are always historically absolute, although none of their manifestations is absolute or exclusive;

the incompleteness of the created world, the fact that it does not stand by itself, the inapplicability of all types of order to borderline cases, the experience of the extreme;

the idea that the ultimate and only refuge is with God.

How pale does all we have said seem beside the religious reality. As soon as we set out to discuss the question, we enter upon the plane of philosophical faith. We are thus led automatically to interpret renewal of religious faith as a return to the primal source, as a renewal of the philosophical faith that is implicit in the religious, as a transformation of religion into philosophy (or philosophical religion). But this, though perhaps it will be the road of a minority, will certainly not be that of mankind.

The philosopher cannot possibly tell the theologians and the churches what to do. The philosopher can only hope to help create the preliminary requirements. He would like to help prepare the ground and to help produce awareness of the intellectual situation necessary for the growth of what he himself cannot create.

What more and more people have been saying for half a century continues to be quickly forgotten, though nearly everyone has been saying it: a new era is arising, in which man, down to the very last individual, is subject to a process of transformation more radical than ever before in history. But since the transformation in our objective living conditions goes so deep, the transformation in our forms of religious belief must go correspondingly deeper in order to mould the new, to fructify and spiritualize it. A change is to be expected in what we have called the matter, the dress, the manifestation, the language of faith, a change as far-reaching as all the other changes that have taken place in our era—or else the eternal truth of Biblical religion will recede beyond the horizon of man; he will no longer experience this truth, and it is impossible to say what might take its place. Hence it is in order, that we do everything in our power to restore the eternal truth; we must plumb its very depths and, unconcerned over what is transient and historical, utter this truth in a new language.

Here the philosopher only becomes involved in questions that he cannot answer, though he knows that the future will assuredly give the answer. Such questions are:

Which dogmas can be dropped because they have actually become alien to modern man and lost their credibility? Even if for the present we say nothing about dropping dogmas, the thinking man must still ask: which dogmas are no longer fully believed even by the professed communicants of the religions?

What solid religious foundation remains?

Is there an element of absurdity that is tenable or even desirable as a content of faith to-day? It would seem that the capacity for the crudest absurdities has if anything been astoundingly intensified in modern man. He succumbs so easily to superstition. But where there is superstition, only faith can conquer, not science. What absurdity might to-day still be the inescapable sign of an authentic faith content?

If all dogmas are to be transformed, by whom will it be done?

Does the fact that the masses of the people continue to attend church services indicate that they gravitate toward an absolute faith? Or must their capacity for devotion to the point of martyrdom be rekindled through new contents that will be found by an uncompromising quest for the truth? Or will it in the end turn out, as Plato thought, that deliberate concealment of the truth by an élite is indispensable in order to educate the masses and preserve even the deepest meanings? Here I believe that the answer is: No. What lies to-day would be indispensable and effective vehicles of truth? Surely there are no such lies.

Again we realize that with such questions we do not strike at the core of the matter. The religious essence itself, inaccessible to the philosopher, must be present in advance. It cannot be construed, it cannot be viewed from outside. The significance of the cult, of rites, of festivals, of dogmatic certainty, of priests, is lost in philosophical discussion. Is this a crucial argument against all philosophy? Is the idea of philosophical faith to-day as in all previous epochs a lifeless illusion? We are told so. But I do not believe it.

What the philosopher has to say of religion is more than inadequate, he does not seem able to touch religion when he discusses it.

Philosophy strives always to broaden its horizon. It extends the scope of its vision from the particular denominational religion to the more comprehensive

Biblical religion, and thence to the truth in all religions. But in so doing it loses precisely that which distinguishes actual religion. While philosophers suppose that by broadening their scope to the universal, they can penetrate the depths of religion, they lose sight of the fact that religions are always bound up with the tangible symbols in which they are embodied. Though they see that such tangible embodiments of the collective and traditional faith are the necessary form of religion, religion remains alien to them because they do not have this faith, and thus are indeed unable to understand what they see.

Philosophy, whether it affirms or combats religion, withdraws from religion in fact, and yet is constantly concerned with it.

(a) Philosophy takes up the cause of the Biblical religion: Western philosophy cannot hide from itself the fact that none of its great philosophers up to and including Nietzsche approached philosophical thought without a thorough knowledge of the Bible. This is no accident. We repeat:

First: Philosophy cannot give man the same thing as religion. Hence it at least leaves the field open for religion. It does not force itself on mankind as the whole and exclusive truth for all men.

Second: Philosophy can scarcely hold its position in the world if the human collectivity does not live in the people through religious faith. Philosophical communication in thought has no compelling force, but only clarifies for the individual man what arises from within himself. Philosophy would be dispersed among fewer and fewer individuals and finally disappear, if the human collectivity did not live by what becomes clear in philosophical faith. Philosophy cannot realize the sociologically effective transmission of the contents indispensable to man, which occurs solely through religious tradition assimilated from early childhood, thus becoming the vehicle also of philosophy.

Third: The contents of the Bible can be replaced for us by no other book.

(b) Philosophy goes beyond Biblical religion: The development of communications, which has brought all the things ever produced on earth into contact with one another, and which has created a need for ever closer understanding among men, has in addition to the Bible revealed to us two other great religious areas: India with the Upanishads and Buddhism, China with Confucius and Lao-tse. The soul of the thoughtful man cannot remain closed to the depth of the truth emanating from these sources. The soul strives to extend its horizons without end.

Here an error is likely to crop up. The Enlightenment sought to find the true religion by assembling the best from all religions. The result however was not the authentic truth, purified of historical accident, but a collection of abstractions watered down by rationalism. The source of this universal faith was in fact only a critical, measuring intelligence. The profound meaning, the poignancy was lost. Trivial generalizations remained.

Since all faith is historical, its truth does not lie in a sum of articles of faith, but in a primal source that is historically manifested in various forms. True, the many religions lead to the one truth, but this truth cannot be attained at one stroke, but only along the roads that were really travelled, roads which cannot be travelled all at once and in the same way.

Hence no rational critique can apprehend this truth. On the contrary, man must, in the context of his own destiny, let the truth be revealed to him as it is uttered through tradition, i.e. he must make it his own. In sounding the depths of the past, one can accomplish this only by being given to oneself through inner action.

With regard to religion, philosophy will in practice approve the following propositions: In order to participate in Biblical religion, one must grow up in the tradition of a definite denomination. Every denomination is good to the extent that the people living in it take possession of the Biblical religion as a whole in spite of the special and finite historical degenerations of the particular historical form. Loyalty and historical consciousness bind me to the denomination in which I awakened. A change of religion is difficult without a breach in the soul. But though in every denominational form of Biblical religion the fixation of faith is determined by the specific time in which it occurs, in individual believers the presence of the full Biblical religion is possible and real. The community of the pious cuts across all denominational lines. And the endless struggles, schisms, and condemnations that have occurred in this field can, in Melanchthon's words, be designated as *rabies theologorum*.

(c) Authority for philosophy: The philosopher is always an individual, he lives at his own risk by drawing upon his own primal depths. But as a man he is part of a whole, and his philosophizing also stands from its very inception in this context.

This context is safeguarded by the secular authority of state and religion. Without authority no human life is possible.

The churches see the necessity of mass guidance, the practical necessity of valid images of reality, of tangible symbols, of an ordered tradition. Their claim to comprehensive truth demands control over the actions of the individual and guidance of his public behaviour. As all-embracing authority for truth, they can, according to their own idea, assimilate all truth, leave room within themselves for all contradictions, everywhere find a synthesis. What no individual can do, because he is finite, particular and one-sided, the church can do as a spokesman for the collectivity.

Again and again the individual rebels against this. In such claims to totality, since they are always raised by men and by no means realize the true totality, he cannot but see a fundamental deception. Though he may recognize an authentic purpose in these claims, he cannot regard the *de facto* authority of the whole as the whole truth. But he for his part, as an individual, cannot realize this truth either. Though in his spiritual efforts he relies on himself, he does not for that reason wish to do away with the church conceived as an embodiment of the universal, as an irreplaceable crystallization of tradition and education, as a form of order. But he strives to prevent it from becoming rigid and exclusive. Consequently he endeavours at his own risk to find the more comprehensive principle by breaking through an actually established universal authority. He seeks living contact with the Comprehensive by striving toward philosophical faith.

This faith however is not invented by him, it is in turn built upon authority. For it grows out of the total tradition of the period extending from the last millennium B.C. to the present day.

Authority is not merely the obedient acceptance of the guidance of an institution and its representatives, the priests, it is also the acceptance, in reverence and trust, of the spiritual guidance of the great past which the last three millennia represent. Here it can truthfully be said: no one can lay a foundation other than that which has been laid from the beginning. It is in this past that we find a proper spiritual climate, a guidance that is authoritative though leaving a margin of indetermination, and that cannot be formulated in objective, universally binding terms.

Any meaningful philosophy must develop in this authority. The danger that this authority will be watered down into general abstractions within reach of the understanding and superficially edifying, in any event existentially empty, is avoided by travelling the historical road: Beginning with his own proximate tradition in family, home country, people, rooted in his own past, the philosopher broadens and deepens it, extending his scope to the vast worlds of the West and thence to all mankind, until finally he consciously finds the pivot of the whole in the epoch between 800 and 200 B.C. Then historical tradition, instead of levelling off in a philosophical system, will become a meaningful whole with its high points, its great men and world, its classical interpretations and its varied articulation in historical development.

Philosophy, always in the form of individual effort, strives to realize universality, to preserve men's openness, to distil the simple, to concentrate it and illuminate it in its unfathomable depths.

Whether such endeavour can contribute any spark, whether the preparatory work of philosophy—which in itself can represent a fulfilment of life for individuals —is to be used in the religions, can be determined by no plan. But in all philosophical effort there lies a tendency to aid religious institutions, whose practical value is affirmed by philosophy, though philosophers cannot directly participate in it.

Chapter Five

PHILOSOPHY AND ANTI-PHILOSOPHY

PHILOSOPHICAL TRUTH IS not the only truth in the world. Up to now it has nowhere been the form of truth in which the majority of men have lived. But philosophical thought is inherently open to every possible mode of life, striving not only to understand it, but also to recognize the truth-meaning it embodies.

Yet at the frontiers of philosophy there is found a mode of living and thinking in which the sources of faith without which philosophy must lose its meaning appear to be abandoned. We call this thinking anti-philosophy when it represents and conceives itself as philosophy, and when it is recognized by others as philosophy. In the cloak of philosophy, anti-philosophy turns against philosophy. Since it signifies the negation of philosophy, philosophical thought must defend itself against it. It is not only an error within philosophical thought, which in that case could be corrected by insight; it is a fundamental error, a complete negation that is thinly disguised as an affirmation by means of substitute constructions. It can be corrected by man self-given and reborn through rediscovering himself in thought. Pseudo-philosophy runs in broad streams through history. Every philosophy must, in transitional phases, succumb to this sham. A philosophically inclined man becomes a philosopher by transcending the anti-philosophy that is always present in himself.

We call unbelief any attitude that asserts absolute immanence and denies transcendence. The question then arises: what is this immanence? Unbelief says: Empirical existence—reality—the world. But empirical existence is only ephemeral presence; unbelief tries to grasp it by affirming becoming and appearance as such. —Reality slowly recedes when I try to know it in itself and as a whole; unbelief tries to get hold of it by absolutizing particular realities.—The world is incomplete, not fully knowable, it is idea; unbelief falsely makes of it an object in a self-contained world system. —In short, unbelief lives in illusion, in isolated realities, in world systems.

Unbelief is never in contact with being, but it cannot avoid admitting in superstitions a substitute for being. It recognizes only immanence, but it cannot avoid asserting a perverted transcendence of this sort.

The numerous varieties of anti-philosophy assume the forms of unbelief. They conceive of themselves as faith or knowledge or intuition. They invoke immediate perceptions and reasons.

I shall choose three examples of philosophical unbelief—demonology, the deification of man, nihilism. We encounter them in both open and concealed forms.

They are so closely interrelated that one form of this unbelief will soon call forth another. They are exceedingly hard to grasp, because they evade definite formulation. In their utterances they make use, unconsciously deceiving themselves and others, of the implements of philosophy. In trying to characterize them, we easily arrive at false definitions, for we try to delimit a chaos that in fact is continuously changing, continuously revealing a different face, for ever contradicting itself, and always ready to attack philosophy at any point. We are facing no clear-cut adversary. In the demonological conception, mystagogy is combined with the idolization of men, to whom the initiates submit, and with nihilism that cancels out all the rest.

The characterizations which I shall attempt are ideal-typical constructions of possibilities that are inherent in us all. But each man is always to a greater degree and primarily the possibility of faith that overcomes these modes of unbelief. And even these modes of unbelief contain some truth, upon which we must finally reflect.

DEMONOLOGY

We call demonology a conception which makes being reside in powers, in effective, form-constituting forces, constructive and destructive, that is in demons, benevolent and malignant, in many gods; these powers are perceived as directly evident, and the perceptions are translated into ideas and formulated as a doctrine. Good and evil alike are hallowed, and the whole is

enhanced by a gazing into dark depths that are manifested in images. The immanent itself is experienced as
passion, power, vitality, beauty, destruction, cruelty.
There is to be sure no transcendence, for in this conception all being is immanent, but this immanence is
not exhausted by the reality accessible to abstract consciousness; it is more than this; in Simmel's words, it
passes as an immanent transcendence, in so far as its
reality does not resolve into the reality that can be
apprehended by the senses and the reason. The para-
doxical term immanent transcendence no longer refers
to things as the possible language of God but as a
power and factor in the world, and a power that is
necessarily split into many forces.

Where man surrenders to these forces, his experience
acquires its enhanced meaning, its radiance, from a
sense of mystery. These forces are perceived with
horror, emotion, spectral shudders, or ecstasy, and
take on a tangible character. The struggle against them
places man himself in the world of the demonic. Sym-
pathy with them, possession with the demon, gives its
irrational impetus to the theory justified by demonology that the forces I follow are necessary, and reinforce
my superstitious belief in the success of my own life
and actions. The longing to return to the mythical age,
the creation of new myths of my own, the thinking in
myths, suffuses the very fundament of my life.

There is an urge in man to come close to the divine,
to experience it directly, as present in the world. This
is accomplished by hallowing all human impulses—it

was a 'god' who did it, not I—and by enchanting the world in the mythical light of the divine.

To-day a good many people have taken to speaking of demons and the demonic. Yet the meanings associated with these words are so varied that a discussion of them may be useful:

(1) *Where a demonological conception was indigenous* it was, like the myth, the historical form of existentially experienced reality. The perception of demons meant an active relation to them, struggle against them, or surrender to them.

Then the great alternative arose for man: to conceive the divine as demonic or to conceive God as transcendence—immanent forces (the many gods) or the one transcendent cause.

At a later date, the demonic forces were integrated into the religious conception of the world; this was done either by transforming them from forces into symbols, a cipher of transcendence, or by a mythical subordination of the demons as angels, messengers and intermediaries of God and the devil. Demonology vanished or was brought under control.

But when demonology is revived in our present-day world, this mythological mode of thought produces only unreal fantasies. It is an illusion to treat demons as realities, to accept them as facts, to 'reckon with' them. There are no demons. Such anti-rational acceptance of so-called experience gives rise to a false interpretation of reality as a sum of forces. This absolutizing of a vague feeling leads to a self-delusion that makes it possible to gain prestige by identifying oneself with demonic forces and, in the confusion of an age made spiritually arid by science, to justify one's actions as dictated by such forces.

If the alternative between demons and God is resolved in no clear decision, a confusion of conception brings confusion into the emotions, the thinking, and the attitude of man.

(2) It is quite a different matter when the demonic serves as an expression for something *unfathomable* that is situated at the *limit of reality*, of my will and being, something that though not actually perceived is nevertheless conceived as an effective entity. Here we no longer have to do with demonologism, but with an imaged expression for something which as a whole we do not understand, something unwilled, perverse, accidental, that exerts an overpowering influence as though from a primal source of its own. Here we no longer have to do with demons, but with the demonic. But this demonic does not take form, does not become a theory; it remains an elusive expression for a border-line condition.

It was in this sense that Goethe used the term demonic and spoke with incomparable penetration of the demonic, but in such a way that its essence remains ungraspable. For it moves only amid contradictions and cannot be conceptually formulated. Hence in Goethe the demonic remains a word with infinitely many meanings, which he applies to that which is not understood, when he wishes to express it as the mystery of an existent, of an occurrence, a causal connection, but can only circle round it with surmises. This is what Goethe, who for a long time had been speaking of demons in multiple meanings as a poetic metaphor, has to say of the demonic:

'It was not divine, for it seemed irrational, not human, for it had no intelligence; not diabolical, for it was beneficent; not angelical, for it often revealed pleasure at people's pain. It resembled chance, for it seemed to break the natural order; it was like providence, for it suggested causal connection. It seemed able to penetrate everything that limits us. . . . It seemed to thrive only on the impossible and to reject the possible with contempt. . . . It constituted a power at cross purposes when not opposed to the ethical world order. . . .

'But this demonic power appears most terrible when it predominates in any man. . . . These are not always the most excellent men, neither in mind nor in talents, they are seldom to be commended for their kindness of heart; but an immense power emanates from them. . . . All moral forces combined are powerless against them, it is in vain that the more lucid among mankind try to cast suspicion upon them as victims of delusion, or swindlers, for the masses are attracted to them. Seldom or never do they encounter their match among their contemporaries, and they can be conquered only by the universe itself, against which they have joined battle.'

(3) Goethe describes the demonic as an objectively

effective power; he circumscribes it by naming its contradictory phenomena. Kierkegaard sees the demonic exclusively in man. Demonic is the man who desires to assert his self absolutely. Kierkegaard elucidates this conception of the demonic by throwing light on the Self and its possible perversion.

'Demonic is that individuality which without intermediary (hence its imperviousness to all others) stands in relation to the idea entirely through himself. If the idea is God, the individuality is religious; if the idea is evil, it is demonic in the narrower sense.'

In so far as the demonic (in this narrower sense) is entirely lucid, it is the Devil. 'The Devil is solely mind and therefore absolute consciousness and lucidity' (it is characteristic for Goethe's wholly different interpretation that Mephisto is not demonic, because he is merely total lucidity of intellect, and negative). But in fact, the demonic in man cannot be lucid. Lucidity arises in the self through its absolute relation to God, not through absolute relation to itself as absolute self.

The demonic and the divine are to be sure incomprehensible: 'Both are silence. Silence is the artifice of the demon, and the greater the silence, the more terrible becomes the demon, but silence is also the testimony of the divine within the individual'; the demonic, like the religious, places man outside the universal. But submersion in the darkness of the demonic has its opposite in boundless illumination before God. To be lost in the demonic paradox is the opposite of being redeemed in the divine paradox.

The demonic as the stubborn adherence to one's contingent self is a desperate desire to be oneself. 'The more consciousness there is in such a man, the more powerful, the more demonic his despair becomes. A man torments himself in some sorrow. He throws his entire passion into this very torment. Now he desires no help. He prefers to rage against everything, he wants to be the man who has been unjustly treated by the whole world, by life. In this despair, he does not even wish to be himself in stoic self-renunciation, he wants to be himself in hatred of the world, himself in his wretchedness. In rebelling against the whole world, he supposes that he has a proof against it, against its goodness. The desperate man imagines that he himself is that proof, and that is what he wants to be, in order to protest against all the world with this torment.'

This demonic will, though intensified by consciousness, cannot become lucid, it can only preserve itself in darkness. Consequently it forces its way into consciousness and at the same time strengthens all the forces of inner occlusion. For it struggles against revelation. Hence the dialectic of revelation and occlusion: 'Occlusion can desire revelation, but it must be accomplished from without, it must befall it. It can desire revelation up to a certain degree, but would like to withhold a certain remnant, so that the occlusion can begin afresh. It can desire revelation, but incognito (in certain poets). Revelation can already have conquered; but at the last moment occlusion ventures a last attempt and is shrewd enough to transform the revelation into mystification, and then it has won the day.' 'The question is whether a man desires to know the truth in the profoundest sense, to let it permeate his whole being, to accept all its consequences, or whether he reserves a last hiding-place for himself in case of need.' The demonic is cunning at self-concealment. For this it makes use of the dialectical, in which it veils itself 'with the demonic virtuosity of reflection.'

Since the demonic has no support in itself, it cannot persevere. For in its occlusion it cannot endure silence, 'and in the end the unfortunate forces his secret upon everyone.' But at the same time he is afraid to reveal himself: 'In confronting one who is superior to him in goodness, the demonic man can plead for himself, he can plead for himself in tears that the other should not speak to him, should not make him weak.'

The true hall-mark of the demonic man, who has withdrawn into his accidental self as into the absolute, is that he can take nothing seriously. 'He does not wish to think seriously of eternity; he is afraid of it, and his fear finds a hundred evasions.'

(4) In the recent period the word demonic has been used vaguely and superficially *for all disturbing things that evade definition*—for the 'irrational'. The unwilled that emerges unexpectedly from the realization of the willed is called 'demonic'. The 'demonism of technology' is the overpowering and seemingly spontaneous reaction arising from the attainment of technological mastery of life. Thus the unconscious is also called demonic, when something that is not and cannot be

clearly understood rises out of the depths of the psychic life of man to dominate him. Helplessness, absence of will, involvement, hopelessness, the sense of being overpowered—all these can call forth the epithet: demonic!

All four of these originally meaningful modes of speaking of the demonic, from mythical objectivization to the mere metaphor, from the belief in a real force in things to an insight into the perversion of man's freedom, have been cut off from their roots and have been absorbed, pell-mell, in modern demonology, which is one of the forms of unbelief. This demonology is as hard to apprehend as Proteus, it is a nothingness that takes on constantly new disguises and in its multiformity makes use of all the old twists of the demonic.

Consequently, philosophy can speak against this demonologism only when it can be defined and held fast for a moment in certain typical experiences. A critique of demonology can then be formulated in the following propositions:

(1) *It misses transcendence*. It is precisely transcendence that demonization with its undue stress on immanent life does not achieve. Without God, only idols remain. The gods themselves have become world. They participate in the impotence of the world, they are under the sway of something other, something absolutely alien, the void.

(2) *Man is lost*. In demonologism freedom is merely the acceptance of the fate that seizes upon man. Man can, to be sure, be happy in the success of his life under

favourable circumstances—with an occasional melancholic recollection of the uncertainty of existence—but when excluded from worldly happiness he is wretched, and in misfortune he can only be empty and despairing. There prevails an inner indifference and matter-of-fact hardness toward the unsuccessful or those smitten by a misfortune from which there is no issue. The individual man has no irreplaceable value. The spirit of humanity is reduced to an inner disposition to behave humanely under certain circumstances, it is not an awe before the soul that is rooted in eternity by its relation to transcendence, before man as such.

(3) *No relation to the one is gained.* There is rather a fragmentation, a diversity of conception. Man splits into his potentialities, taking up one to-day and another to-morrow—life becomes forgetfulness. Life with the demons becomes a flux, a dissolution in the indeterminate. This unbelief cannot be grasped in its authentic meaning, for it interprets itself always differently. In it we are at the mercy of the stream of impulses and passions that rend us to pieces. Everything can be justified. Despite the power of the given moment, continuity is lacking. Despite the intensity of the affirmation, inner concentration is lacking.

The ascent to the transcendence of the one has always been accomplished through the conquest of demonology. Socrates wrested himself away from the demons in order to follow his *daimonion* and in it the divine commandment. The prophets conquered the worship of Baal, in order to serve God.

(4) *Demonology is submerged in nature*. Nature is regarded as the ultimate, all-embracing necessity. The beasts are demonic. And man feels demonic in so far as he is like a beast. Where demonologism is dominant, man loses his sense of distinction from nature. When things go relatively well, demonologism takes the form of trust in nature. But trust in nature is not trust in God. When the trust in nature is frustrated, what is left of it loses its moorings. Trust in nature becomes idolatry, such as was once practised throughout the world in the nature cults.

(5) *Modern demonology is purely an aesthetic attitude*. Characteristic of this is the irresponsibility of demonic thought. It is contemplation of supposed reality, rather than fulfilment of one's own reality. It is an escape into aestheticism accompanied by an obscure desire for the indeterminate as the medium best suited to a perverse self-assertion. This makes possible passion as momentary emotion, but bars the way to the passion of the life-sustaining, unswervingly persevering decision. Here it becomes possible to demand a decision between good and evil, but to reduce any such decision to impotence by recognizing evil in the tragic. A constant confusion between the ethical and aesthetic is made possible. First one speaks with moral pathos of good and evil, then aesthetically of the demonic. Whenever a situation is without issue, one is permitted to leap from the ethical to the aesthetic. Man no longer need commit himself, because for every situation he has a stock of aesthetic images with their illusory grandeur.

Life is fragmented into the multiplicity of the contingent.

(6) *Demonology sets up an intermediary form of being that is neither empirical reality nor transcendent actuality.* It strives to apprehend reality but misses it, deluding itself instead with a supposed supersensory sphere: even the knowable becomes obscured. It desires the supersensory, but misses it in the belief that it is immanent: it loses God. But everything that is not either world (as demonstrable reality) or God is deception and illusion, and particularly when our urge for edification and sensation is divided into a torrent of passion and intoxication. There is God and the world and nothing in between. All realities can be the language or messengers of God, by virtue of their symbolism, but there are no other gods beside God, there are no demons. The essential here is how I discern the finger of God at the limits of reality. What thrusts itself between me and God, appears to be materialistic folly or godless raving.

DEIFICATION OF MAN

For men to heap fulsome reverence on an individual man, to elevate him to the superhuman, to see the ideal of humanity realized in him, is a universal phenomenon. Men tend to submit blindly to such an individual, to expect wonders of him. Consider for example that motion picture stars must travel incognito to avoid being crushed by the crowds, or that Gandhi was obliged to protect himself systematically from '*darshan* seekers' (*darshan* means the sight of a saint). And in centuries gone by when kings showed themselves to the people, the sick were cured.

The deification has its effects on the man who is deified: men torment the man they regard as holy to make him act in accordance with their ideal. They expect him to submit, they exhibit him, as it were, and he must be available. There is in the masses an avidity for a cult of man. As though the object of deification conferred a certain tranquillity by his mere presence, just as the queen bee keeps the hive in order by her presence.

The most evident form of human power is represented by rulers and generals. The self-will and general indiscipline of men leads to the appearance of the tyrant who does violence to them all. He who does not obey the law out of freedom, succumbs to the compulsion to obey an external force. And then the astonishing thing occurs. The tyrant, this instrument of evil for the restraint of evil, becomes an object of deification. Alexander, Caesar, Napoleon and others make their way through history as idols. They were indeed men extraordinary for their tiger-like energy, their presence of mind, their unerring realism, their memory, industry, and instinct for everything conducive to domination and power. Even in their lifetime they were magnified, either in that they declared themselves to be God or the son of God, or acceded to the desires of the crowd and used them as an instrument of power. The tyrants become gods. Alexander became the son of God, the Roman god-emperors enforced the official state cult of their numen. Even where this superstition is cast off, we are still confronted with manifestations of irrational obeisance, and we see human idols as an object of secular veneration. It is always extraordinary how easily the actual facts concerning the deified individuals are evaded, veiled, reinterpreted.

And tyrants are not the only men to be deified. Many an ancient philosopher was demonized or hero-ized. To-day, in a world of fading cultural values, there is a remnant of this attitude in the blind veneration that is accorded to great men and charlatans. Both are looked upon as absolutely unassailable. The tendency to make myths of such figures is ineradicable.

It is true that a man will not readily proclaim himself as a god, unless he is mad or does so for political pur-poses. He is more likely to claim the unique distinction of speaking God's message. He alone is called to do so, and this gives him a claim to the reverence of men.

The deification of man is also a factor in the shaping of great religions. But the interpretation then is such that there is no deification of man at all. The case in question is differentiated from all other instances of the deification of man, which is condemned as such.

Why the deification of man?

There is in man an inclination to seek a perfect man who will in a sense be for him what he himself would like to be but cannot.

The deification of man cannot dispense with an

authority in the world toward whom absolute obedience (not relative obedience to laws, officials, institutions) is possible in the sense of obedience to God; it rests on the need for the physical, tangible proximity of the distant, hidden God.

Sometimes the deification of man functions as a substitute for faith, an absurd faith that tries to regard itself as authentic. Most characteristic of this actual unbelief is perhaps its insistence that all men believe in its object; it is fanatical, unloving, angry, it finds it intolerable that others should not have the same faith. Let all men worship what I worship.

Fundamentally, the deification of man is one kind of demonology. As the godless seize upon demons as a supposed transcendence, so do they also seize upon living men and make gods of them.

Regardless of the motives with which the deification of man is associated, regardless what sublime forms and profound interpretations it may take on, it is at the root a fallacy. Philosophical faith unmasks it in every form. It never for a moment forgets the finiteness and unfinished character of man. It holds firmly to God's commandment not to confound His identity, not to snatch him by means of falsehoods out of the concealment to which he will only return the more resolutely. It demands of man that he dare to stand immediately before Him and await what He will say. Man should not withdraw from Him, by conceiving a man as an absolute, by listening to that man instead of God or as though he were God. Man is subject to the hard com-

mandment to bear up with the world's emptiness, in
the realization that God is not present like something
or other in the world. Only in this austere situation is
man free to hear God when God speaks, only then does
he remain ready, even if God should not speak, only
then does he remain open to the reality that is historically manifested to him.

There is in the world no man capable of being God
for us, but there are men whose freedom in hearing
God encourages us by showing us what is possible for
men. We cannot seize the hand of God in the flesh, but
we can seize the hand of our companion in fate.

The deification of man dishonours man by making
things easy for him. It gives him the tangible, whereas
it is his situation in the world that he must do without
this tangibility, and instead find only hieroglyphs and
images along the road by which he can, and hence
should, come to himself through God.

NIHILISM

While demonology and the deification of man offer
a substitute for faith, open unbelief is known as nihilism. The nihilist ventures to appear without disguise.
For him all contents of faith are untenable, he has
unmasked all interpretations of the world and of being
as delusions; for him everything is conditional and
relative; there is no fundament, no absolute, no being
as such. Everything is questionable. Nothing is true,
everything is permissible.

Nihilism can only exist in one who lives by impulses of vitality, love of life, will to power. By affirming these, nihilism cancels itself out in favour of a vital faith.

Or it is really serious in its experience of the void. I can feel nothing, love nothing, respect nothing. My soul is empty. The nihilistic idea justifies me in this, tells me that I am right.

Or a boundless disappointment causes me to experience the collapse of everything in which I have believed—the disloyalty of one I loved, the betrayal of the state leadership, the falsity of statements proclaimed as authoritative. The course of the world shows how everything that once was accepted as true vanishes in illusion. The nihilistic idea sets out to prove to me that my experience is no special experience, but reveals the whole of being.

But the nihilistic idea can negate only when it starts from something recognized, measured by which nothingness, disillusionment, betrayal, the lie, illusion are disclosed. In order to speak, nihilism requires a fundament which, if really apprehended, would cancel out nihilism in favour of the positive value represented by this fundament. Consequently, the method of radical nihilism consists in first rejecting everything on the basis of standards regarded as self-evident, and then causing everything to vanish in a single whirl of reciprocal negation.

Let us examine a few examples of nihilistic negation:

(1) *There is no God.*—For the existence of God, the creator of the world, is not proved, there is not even a

suggestion of a proof to show that it is even possible or probable.

The premise of this negation is the validity of what is here recognized as the possibility of proof, to wit, factual statements about something present in the world, and rational proofs of finite things by finite means. Hence this negative idea treats questions of transcendence like questions dealing with finite things in the world; and it does not even touch upon what is intended in statements about God, since it takes their content as a factual statement about something present in the world.

(2) *There is no relationship between God and man.*—For such a connection cannot be experienced and is not experienced, because there is no God. What is represented as such experience rests on psychological delusions and the mistaken interpretation of experience.

The premise in this negation is the factuality of experience in the world. It is hypostatized as Being *per se*, particularly in the form of empirical knowledge that the temporal and spatial process reveals a recurrent, regular pattern. But the existential experience of freedom is denied.

(3) *There is no obligation toward God.*—For this obligation is in fact only subjection to laws and decrees existing in the world. Here obedience is possible, contingent upon the power and prestige of the authorities in question.

The premise in this negation is the absolute character of such authorities in the world. It is on the basis of this premise that the profound, absolute, life-sustaining obligation is denied, which can nowhere find so comfortable a support in the decrees and laws of man.

These examples reveal a positivistic nihilism. It seems to regard being as identical with empirical existence, which can be fully known, in the trivial sense of this term. But if there is nothing, then this empirical existence, in so far as it is posited as absolute, is also nothing. On the basis of such positivism, nihilism concerns itself with the ordering of human life, under the presupposition that such an order can be derived from the knowledge of empirical realities.

For example: sex relations are to be regulated according to principles of hygiene with a view to realizing the aim of a happy life, without further religious or ethical considerations. The premise here is the absolute character of a mere life. But it is untenable for two reasons: 'happiness' cannot be clearly defined (not to mention its fragility in every form), and positivistic regulation is in fact unsuccessful.

In these cases nihilism, at first concealed, makes its appearance only when the uncritically accepted latent premise (namely, that our horizon is limited to empirical knowledge, current value judgments, efficient technical devices) becomes conscious and hence untenable. The negations are then retained but in addition the minimum of truth that is always premised in the negations is also negated. Again we have the whirlpool, again there is no firm ground but only the meaningless vitality of the moment, with its unthinking immediacy;

man is surrendered to the natural process, to the level of which nihilism, in simplifying itself, descends.

Quite different from this nihilism, which might be called the nihilism of the Philistines, is the nihilism originating in horror at the reality of the world and of human life. The idea of God itself—the idea of God and goodness, love, truth and omnipotence—becomes a standard by which to condemn God and the world.

If God desired truth—this line of thought runs—He would have created man and the world differently. Hence God is either not omnipotent or not good.

Throughout history we hear the desperate accusations of man against God. It is not God but an evil demon to which this world owes its existence. And in nihilism these accusations collapse: the object of accusation is lacking, there is neither God nor evil demons, things are as they are—there is nothing but this worthlessness and deviltry of human existence.

Interrelation of the three forms of unbelief: Demonology, the deification of man, and nihilism belong together. Just as the true is oriented toward the one, even though the one truth is never visible, so does the fragmentation of anti-philosophy seem to arrive at an analogy of the one, in so far as in it the positions reciprocally produce one another.

Nihilism is intolerable. It seeks evasions in demonology and deification of man. Here it finds a footing. But the nihilistic climate remains. Hence there is in the area of demonology a kind of urge toward nothingness, a conjuring of forces out of the void.

Where man is hardened to the nothingness and does not despair, life becomes a life without hope. There is either poverty of soul and insensibility, or a pretension of heroism, which, however, since it knows itself and deliberately acts itself out, is only a heroistic gesture, not existence.

The deification of man is a kind of escape from nihilism, yet is itself covertly nihilistic. It must lead to disillusionment when the deified man is living and visible, a contemporary. Then the realization that the man is after all nothing but a man, drives one all the more resolutely into nihilism. And from the outset, the deification of one man serves as a means of despising all others. These others are denied all rights, are used as material and expended.

Truth in each of the three forms: It is the task of philosophy not only to reject, but at the same time to acknowledge the truth in what has been rejected.

Demonology contains a kernel of truth, namely, that on the empirical plane transcendence cannot be perceived directly but only in signs which need to be decoded. The feeling that sensible reality has a non-sensible substratum, that the face of things and events points to a hidden meaning, is not without justification. Mythological categories contain a truth that strikes us with irresistible evidence when the chaff is separated from the grain. To ignore this truth, is to impoverish one's soul, to create a vacuum. A man who has lost his ear for such language seems no longer capable of love. For if the transcendent has become entirely nonsensuous, it no longer holds for him an object of love. It may be true that such an abstraction can supply nourishment to a unique love in the empirical world, and that a love so nourished remains pure and is safe from error. But deprived of a tangible, sensuous expression of the transcendent, man also runs the risk of losing himself in the worldless, the inhuman, the alien. Although demonology is untrue, man can and should discern the speech of God in His images and hieroglyphs and should not be deterred by the fact that in objectivizing formulation, this speech is utterly ambiguous. It is not only the weakness of our finite nature, but also our love of the world as the creation of God, that forbids us to root ourselves exclusively in a sensual transcendence, except in extreme transitional cases.

The deification of man contains in distorted form the truth that in the world the only authentic thing for man is man. There is something in man that makes it possible to say that God created man in His image; but that man fell away from God and consequently in every man as man the image of God is veiled. Great men are for those who come after them orientation and model, object of veneration and possible road to resurgence, even though they remain men with their deficiencies and failures, and hence can never be an object of imitation. It is a free relation of man to man when for the individual there exists a life-sustaining historical bond with certain individuals, grounded in tradition and fulfilled in love.

In *nihilism* something is expressed that the man of

integrity cannot overlook. In the reality of the world, despair is inevitable in extreme situations. Every faith must explore the possibility of nothingness. No faith may arrogate to itself a certainty on which objective reliance can be placed. Since faith is always a risk, a gift, it must be constantly aware of the nihilistic threat, lest it succumb to the temptation of pride, to which it so often has succumbed when it has become ossified.

Nihilism differs from the demonology and deification of man into which it escapes: manifest nihilism is irrefutable, just as conversely no faith is demonstrable. Those who, when confronted by the terrible absurdities and injustices of the world, do not acknowledge them in their full reality, but pass over them with an almost automatic matter-of-factness by means of talk about God, sometimes seem less concerned with the truth than the nihilist himself. Dostoievsky speaks of the torture and murder of innocent children. What kind of being, world, God is it, which makes this possible and permitted? The man who has suffered horror and who for ever after goes through the world with hate and indignation, and lust for revenge, is assuredly the most difficult neighbour. He himself in turn inspires fear and horror. Against him rise up the instincts of self-preservation that would destroy him like a madman. Just as a man can fall into madness through nature, so through other men can he fall into this horror that makes him completely nihilistic. We do not assent to this, we do not recognize that he has this right, but declare that evil remains evil even when it occurs as a continuation and reaction to a preceding evil. But we become unable to believe in a harmony of being. Boundless pity, silent perplexity, hopelessness must overcome us. It is more justified to ask: how is it possible that we do not all of us become nihilists?—than to overlook the experiences that can lead to nihilism.

And yet all my lectures are an attempt to ward off nihilism. I speak precisely of what I have just seemed to reject, I speak of God. Hence my reserve. I have nothing to proclaim. Each of my listeners retains the right to examine for himself, not simply to follow the statements of the lecturer, but rather to take them as an encouragement to strive for his own certainty.

And so I venture to say once again that demonology, the deification of man and nihilism carry out in different ways the same fallacy, the fallacy of attempting to apprehend the truth at one stroke that misses the goal. In the presence of the single proposition: God is, the whole fallacy must vanish like mist beneath the sun. But the mist presses upon us, for in short-sighted attempts to grasp it we apprehend something tangible, concrete, visible—while if the truth remains intangible and invisible, it seems to dissolve into nothingness. Thus we can reach the truth only by the detour of worldliness, we succumb again and again to those fallacies, and only in transcending them are we able to perceive the depth of our authentic being, of godhead.

God is the most remote of all things, he is transcendence; all attempts to absolutize anything else are mere shortsightedness. But what God, transcendence is, can be discussed indefinitely, can be circumscribed with negations, but never really apprehended.

CONNECTION BETWEEN PHILOSOPHY
AND ANTI-PHILOSOPHY

Faith is attained through unfaith. He who does not know the experience of unbelief, cannot attain a faith that is conscious of itself.

The same is true of anti-philosophy. It must not be simply discarded. It is not something superfluous, accidental, negligible. It is a frontier region of philosophy, and a transition within philosophy. But it is at the same time something that is rejected in being transcended.

Transcendence seems to be accessible by all roads. There is truth on the roads of anti-philosophy, yet each of them leads to a special fallacy: demonology to the fallacy of superstition and aestheticism; deification of man to the fallacy of confusing God and man; nihilism to the despairing, hating, emptiness of a contingency dissolving in chaos.

All three can as transition, as language, or as a spur, perform a function of truth, but in becoming definitive and fixed, they turn to fallacy.

So far we have spoken of contents of unbelief as an antithesis to philosophy. But the instruments of nihilistic and of dogmatic anti-philosophy are categories which are rooted in the very nature of the matter, which appear inevitably and require methodical and conscious elucidation. A logical discussion of the philosophical modes of thought, which are a methodically developed transcending, and of the modes of object thinking and fixation on which philosophy runs aground, would have to show what truth is and what form it takes.

The truth is simple, the false is manifold. The truth has coherence, the false is scattered. The truth is infinite, the false is endless. Truth builds upon itself, the false destroys itself.

Truth is the primal source of our thinking and the measure of the false. An inventory of the possibilities of the false could be drawn up only by the guidance of the true, from which it arises through adulteration, perversion, transposition. Here we shall give no such inventory, but only a tentative list of the forms of anti-philosophy.

(1) *Absolutization:* The fallacy consists in isolating and positing as absolute something that is valid at one level of being or of thinking, that is valid from certain points of view and in certain respects, that has particular validity.

Since knowledge is always circumscribed in meaning, since furthermore all proof presupposes a reference to a finite thing within the world, statements on being as a whole, e.g. concerning the world as such, are false, in so far as statements standing unequivocally by themselves, demonstrable, and having a definitive meaning are in question. Demonstrable is only the indemonstrability of universal statements, e.g. concerning the world as a whole, whether they be negative or positive.

(2) *Ontology:* Ontology purports to be a doctrine of being itself as such and as a whole. In practice, however, it inevitably becomes a particular knowledge of something within being, not a knowledge of being itself.

In truth there is only the elucidation of the Comprehensive; this elucidation is never completed, never definitive, it leaves a margin of indeterminacy; and there is a universal methodology and system of categories of the intelligible. Both take the place of ontology, which always passes by the truth.

Ontology, even when it includes God, is ultimately a doctrine of immanence, of the subsisting, not of Being but of the Existent, in so far as it is known by man. True philosophy must not be confused with this ontological perversion of philosophical elucidation. Philosophy does not leave the area of the Comprehensive, does not forget the process of transcending that is inseparable from it, remains open to the being that cuts across time, the being that thought apprehends as the actual presence of eternity in historicity.

(3) *Empty reflection:* This is the name we give to the thinking which progresses endlessly, carried along by the abstract categories, without reference to contents. Reflection questions, but only in the movement of negation, shunning immersion in the primal source and thus never transcending itself. Thus it merely dissolves all the given, all fixed goals. This endless annihilation

may, for example, take the form of a superficial accusing irony, understandable from psychological motives; it is unconscious of, and indifferent to, its own origin.

(4) *Dogmatic professions of faith:* Since all existential relations to transcendence are dialectical, any definite statement is false as regards immediate content. Certainty is found in dialectical movement, not in securing the title deed of a thing through logical formulation.

When creeds are made absolute, they become a kind of banner. They are the rallying points, the sign of membership in a group, the badge of an enthusiasm, a battle emblem.

(5) *The credo quia absurdum:* The premises of formal logic are valid only in the sphere of the knowable, i.e. with regard to ideal mathematical objects or cogent experimental insights. It can be shown philosophically that this knowledge does not exhaust being: this is done through the antinomies, through speculative expression in paradoxes.

But it is both false and reckless to attempt expression in the forms of object knowledge of the empirically or logically impossible as a truth postulated by religion. Such an attempt results in a complete perversion of meaning. Instead of asserting objective unfathomableness, we assert the positive impossibility of an object that is defined in words; in the name of openness to extreme horizons, thought disavows itself; the ability to hear (which is a mark of love of truth) is replaced by a *sacrificium intellectus* (which marks contempt for truth).

These forms of anti-philosophy exemplify peculiar transpositions, toward which we are at all times inclined:

(1) *The fanaticism for truth that becomes untrue:* As the darkness from which we emerge is illumined, we develop a desire for unlimited integrity. We feel impelled to elucidate, justify, motivate everything. There is nothing that should not be questioned and examined. An enthusiastic love for truth is willing to run any risk just for the sake of truth.

But this impulse seldom remains pure. The love of truth becomes associated with a sense of superiority and power, and soon there develops a combativeness, a desire to destroy and torment. Hate exploits seeming love of truth as a weapon.

This occurs all the more easily because the question of the meaning of truth—a question by no means easy to answer—is in this case from the very outset unclarified, indeed unasked. And so an amazing thing happened: the man of the Enlightenment became insincere. He could hypocritically invoke truth, while fighting for earthly interests, and was able to pour forth bathos about the truth in neurotic helplessness.

In particular, inauthentic fanaticism for the truth presupposes pseudo-axioms, which take various forms according to the situation, for example: the world could be well ordered provided there were clear understanding and good will; the truth can have only good and desirable consequences; one must tell the truth under all circumstances and at all times. Or conversely, after disillusionments, one might say: the world is corrupt; truth is useless, it merely destroys; one must conceal the truth and find the expedient, useful lie. Thus fanaticism for the truth attains its climax when out of supposed integrity it favours the lie. Such false total assertions serve in fact as an escape from authentic effort in behalf of the truth.

(2) *The abandonment of dialectical circling:* On the basis of formal alternatives, a tendency arises, instead of realizing the meaning of an idea with all its tensions, polarities, dialectical movements, to apprehend it in a straight, pragmatic line. The consequence of this is not merely that one misses the goal, but life itself is paralyzed.

This can be understood on various levels of analogy. The psycho-physical process is itself a circular process, the rudiments of whose structure have already been disclosed to research: in the psycho-physical functions of motor activity, speech, locomotion, work, perception, respiration, evacuation, sexuality. Where the purposive will and with it attention intervenes, there can it is true be an increase in activity, but there can also be a radical disturbance. For the circular process, the letting oneself go in activity, the passive in the active, must always remain the foundation.—In the psychological sphere, there is a continuous union of opposites. The voluntary occurs only in the involuntary, tension only along with relaxation, the conscious thought process only with the unconscious collaboration of inspiration. Where a state of activity occurs without relaxation, the result is hysteria. The will itself conceals within it that which cannot be willed, for realization it requires that which it does not will. I cannot will will.—In the existential sphere man is himself only when he is given to himself in his selfness. Freedom is a self-bestowal by transcendence. This freedom is not expedience, not obedience to a calculated duty, not forced activity, but a will detached from all compulsion, and this will is transcendent necessity.—Thus psycho-physical order, psychological naturalness, existential freedom, are modes of realization which cannot be apprehended in terms of clear-cut alternatives. Whatever our conscious-ness strives to attain in rectilinear purposiveness re-mains dependent upon them.

The sacrifice of this fundament in favour of rational fixations of finite goals, arises from lack of courage, from unwillingness to run risks, from the intellect's love of comfort, from a need to find security in the un-equivocal, from the habit of violent short-cuts incul-cated in us by modern psychology. Then we seek a refuge at the point where life ceases and the void menaces, and it is there precisely that our intellect pre-sumes to find the most reliable hold.

(3) *The confusion of the Comprehensive with its particular objectivization:* Philosophical thought arises from an in-ward disposition of the soul to strive for self-aware-ness in thought, hence for objectivity and communi-cation.

In our understanding of philosophical writings, it is essential that we partake of this basic aspiration.

We must through thinking come to this fundament which is the Comprehensive principle, by which thought came into being, but which itself can never be an adequate object of thought. This fundament can be discerned by philosophical appropriation: in its depth and plenitude, in its emptiness and scantiness, in its fragility and distortion. It is a fundamental fallacy to confuse the tangible content of ideas, their definite objects, the sensible character of the existent—to confuse all these particulars with the Comprehensive. It is only with the Comprehensive that authentic communication, attraction and repulsion, begin. Everything susceptible to objective statement is on the other hand merely the language of the underlying seeking attitude, and as mere language, it turns to nothingness when the source from which it arose vanishes. Thus man can delusively fill his emptiness with a language that is merely handed down, and a position contingent on the practical interests of the moment can make a resplendent but illusory cloak of old ideas.

Philosophical thought grows out of the Comprehensive. Anti-philosophy stands always on the solid ground of a particularity and objectivity that it chooses at will. It falls from the fluid equilibrium of living philosophy into the stable banality of rational directness, or evaporates in vague enthusiasm.

With this I conclude my discussion of the anti-philosophy which we reject but in which we are nevertheless always involved—against which we remain defenceless if we do not consciously know it—which we do not despise but which we must look in the face in order to know ourselves—and for this reason we must never over-confidently suppose that we have overcome it.

Chapter Six

THE PHILOSOPHY OF THE FUTURE

PHILOSOPHY STRIVES TO apprehend eternal truth. Is this truth not always the same, the one and whole truth? Perhaps—but we do not gain possession of it in an unequivocal and universally valid form. Being reveals itself to us only in time, the truth is revealed only in its temporal manifestation. But the complete truth is not objectively accessible in time. Neither man as an individual, nor history can apprehend it otherwise than in ephemeral manifestations.

As an individual, each of us reaches the end of his life without really knowing what is. He achieves nothing definitive, but remains on a road which merely breaks off and ends in no absolute goal.

The labour of philosophy is a kind of parable for all our activity. Just as we come to the point where we can really start philosophizing, says Kant, we must leave the whole business in the hands of the beginner. That is what every philosopher who has not congealed in the possession of the truth must feel when he grows old. It is the feeling of intellectual youth in the sorrow of leave-taking.

But is life for the future the essential import of our work? I do not believe so. For we serve the future only in so far as we realize the present. We must not expect the authentic only from the future. Even though this presentness cannot in fact attain to durable consummation, in which I can rest and endure in time, it is nevertheless possible in penetrating this actuality to penetrate in a sense the eternal present in its temporal manifestation. The actuality of the truth in time is, to be sure, as impossible to capture as an optical image—but it is always with us.

Thus our life in history is two things at once: the life that serves, and creates a basis for, the life of those to come after us—and the life that cuts across history, the life in actuality as such, oriented toward transcendence, that liberates us.

This liberation in its completeness erases time. But if there is such liberation, it is incommunicable, except in art or in the speculative idea, or in the religious cult, or in lofty moments of harmony between two human beings—and in every case it is questionable for subsequent reflection, that knows only of its outward manifestation.

If history is the revelation of being, the truth is present in history at all times and never, it is always in movement, and it is lost when it appears to have become a definitive possession. Perhaps the truth is most profoundly manifested where the movement is characterized by the greatest upheaval. To-day we can attempt in the light of the past, to achieve awareness of the specific conditions that determine our lives and the future. The questions arise: Are we to-day involved in a profound revolutionary transition? Are we moving into a world of new possibilities? Are we faced with challenges raised by this very situation?

We all of us are aware that our era has altered the course of history more radically than any other era known to us. It seems comparable to the unknown age in which the first fire was kindled, in which tools were invented, in which the earliest states were established. The new facts are: modern technology with its consequences for man's working methods and for society— the unity of the globe created by modern communications, which have made the earth smaller than for example the *orbis terrarum* of Roman days—the absolute limit represented by the smallness of our planet— the antinomies of freedom and effective action, personality and mass, world order and imperium—the crucial importance of the increased population, transformed from nations into masses, seemingly enabled to understand and participate in developments, but actually transformed into slaves to be made use of—the breakdown of all past ideals of order and the need for finding a new human order to save us from mounting chaos— the questionableness of all traditional values, which must prove themselves or be changed—and further: the concrete political situation, determined by the world powers, the United States and Russia—an internally torn Europe, diminishing in size and thus far unable to find itself—the awakening of the vast masses of Asia, on their way to becoming crucial factors of political power.

The course of events has led us from an era of bourgeois contentment, progress, education, which pointed to the historical past as proof that it had achieved security, into an age of devastating wars, mass death and mass murder (accompanied by an inexhaustible generation of new masses), of the most terrible sense of menace, an age in which humanity is being extinguished and chaotic disintegration seems to be the master of all things.

Is all this a spiritual revolution, or is it an essentially external process, arising from technology and its consequences?—A catastrophe and an immense, as yet unclear possibility, something which will be merely destructive until man awakens and becomes able to react to it, until, instead of unconsciously renouncing, he discovers himself amid the utterly new conditions of his existence?

The picture of the future is more uncertain and unclear, but perhaps both more promising and more hopeless than ever before. If I am aware of the task of humanity, not with regard to the immediate requirements of existence, but with regard to eternal truth, I must inquire concerning the state of philosophy. What should philosophy do in the present world situation?

To-day there is a *de facto* nihilism in numerous forms. Men have appeared, who seem to have abandoned all inwardness, for whom nothing seems to have any value, who stagger through a world of accident from moment to moment, who die with indifference and kill with indifference—but who seem to live in intoxicating quantitative conceptions, in blind interchangeable fanaticisms, driven by elemental, irrational, overpowering and yet quickly passing emotions, and ultimately by the instinctual urge for the pleasure of the moment.

If we listen to the words that are uttered amid this tumult, they seem like a veiled preparation for death. Mass education has made men blind and thoughtless, capable of everything in their drunkenness, until finally they accept death and killing, mass death in mechanized warfare as a matter of course.

But the most lucid philosophy also aims at enabling man to face death. Philosophy seeks to find a basis on which death is to be sure not intellectually accepted, but borne in the turmoil of suffering, not with stoicism, but with a loving and confident imperturbability.

It is seldom that either is successful in a pure form. This nihilism lives by mystifications, the unmasking of which exposes man to despair, unless all has previously been lost in dull indifference. And this philosophy is no secure possession, it must be achieved each day anew, and abandons one again and again. The result is an intermediary state between nihilism and philosophy— a man who has not entirely succumbed to nihilism but does not yet partake of philosophy. And here frightening situations arise. I shall cite two examples, occurring in the year 1938.

As was then the style, a young man was speaking of

the empire that was to be founded. He seemed to be full of enthusiasm. I interrupted him with the question: What meaning has this empire and the war that is expected to lead to it? Answer: Meaning? No meaning at all! Those are just things that are coming. What can have meaning is at most that in a battle I bring my thirsty comrade water at the risk of my life.

On 9 November 1938, a student, who was a SA leader, took part in the anti-Jewish pogrom. He told his mother about it. He had carried out the action as mildly as possible. In one house he took up a plate, threw it crashing to the floor, and cried out to his comrades: I hereby state that this house is demolished, and left it without having demolished it. But he went on to relate that the day had made a great and encouraging impression upon him; he had seen what forces lie dormant in the people and of what the people were capable; this seemed hopeful for a coming war. He expounded the new ethic and the greatness of the Führer. His terrified mother interrupted him: My boy, you don't believe that yourself. For a moment he was speechless, but then said resolutely: No, I don't believe it, but one has to believe it.

The first young man found a footing in the simplest humanity, darkened however by the imperial climate, even though he saw through its nullity. The second took seriously the saying: What matters is not what you believe, but that you believe. This is a wonderful perversion. Faith becomes a faith in faith. To this correspond a number of attitudes that attempt to be nihilistic and positive at the same time: One wants to be brave and dispense with all meaning, hence one represents a calculated meaninglessness as meaning. One preaches 'useless service' as an accomplishment—the sacrifice of everything, but for nothing—one preaches the impassioned affirmation of anything at all, fanatical determination for nothing. One seizes upon old words like honour, patriotism, loyalty, but at the same time sacrifices everything to the machine, to orders from above, to terror, thus showing that all those words were mere props. One develops an iron mask, within which one remains tense, always at the edge of explosion, an absolute without content.

There are many beaten tracks of escape from this despair:

One sings the praises of 'dynamism' at any price, one exults in motion as such, one desires the new and the destruction of the old. One admires all the great men of violence: Genghis Khan, Shih Huang Ti, Agathocles, and those who have always been admired: Alexander, Caesar, Napoleon.

Or conversely, one praises the return to the past. The primitive as such has charm and eternal truth, whether one is referring to the prehistoric era or to the lives of modern primitive peoples. Or one admires the Middle Ages, the great static orders, the empires that imposed their style upon centuries.

One strives for a new myth, sets up a crude one in the dictatorial movements, or a more sublime one in educated circles which make a cult of Hölderlin, van

Gogh (or even of their epigones). Here it is forgotten that those great men were wonderful exceptions, that in most cases their authenticity was bound up with ruinous madness. The real mythical presence in them is extraordinarily impressive in this unmythical modern world. Hölderlin's pure soul is indeed unforgettable, its myth is enchanting, to enter into its sphere is a joy. But all this is no true myth, it is authentic only in these individuals, it has no bridge to society, and hence suddenly becomes as nothingness.

And there is always the beaten track of the religious denominations. When everything is confounded in the whirl of unmeaning, they show their steadfastness. In accordance with the freedom-shunning spirit of the times, they alternate between anarchy and dictatorship, revealing to-day their unlimited orthodoxy, their aim of commanding man's complete fealty—but without being able to restore what religion once was: a force pervading the whole of life and all everyday life, from birth to death—the sphere in which everything happens and by virtue of which man is always at home. To-day religion, too, has become a special sphere, a Sunday aside from and outside of normal life.

These religions with their alternative 'either nihilism or revelation' reject philosophy. Philosophy is reproached as sharing the guilt for the evil of the modern soul, as its intellectual instigator.

But it is not only from those who wish to force us into revealed faith with their alternative, that we hear about the end of philosophy. The end of philosophy was proclaimed also by the National Socialists, who could not tolerate the independence of philosophical thought. Philosophy was to be replaced by biology and anthropology. And in addition, every form of nihilism condemns philosophy as a world of illusion, of vain dreams, of feeble self-deceptions. For nihilism, both religion and philosophy are at an end. Only the man without illusions, without roots and without aim, is regarded as free. Furthermore, there is a widespread public opinion which looks on philosophy as at least superfluous; for philosophy is held to be blind to the present, its forces and movements. What is the use of Philosophy? it is asked. Philosophy does not help. Plato was unable to help the Greeks, he didn't save them from going under, in fact he contributed indirectly to their decline.

All negations of philosophy originate in something outside of philosophy, either in some definite content of faith that might be endangered by philosophy, or in practical aims for which philosophy is useless, or in a nihilism that rejects everything, and hence also philosophy, as worthless.

But in philosophical effort something takes place that is not seen by all those who reject it: in it man rediscovers his primal source. In this sense, philosophy is absolute and without aim. It can neither be justified through something else, nor on the basis of utility for any purpose. It is not a girder to support us or a straw to grasp at. No one can have philosophy at his disposal. No one can use it as a means.

We venture to assert that philosophy cannot cease as long as men are living. Philosophy upholds the aspiration to attain the meaning of life beyond all worldly purposes—to make manifest the meaning that embraces all these purposes—cutting in a sense across life to fulfil this meaning by actual realization—to serve the future by our own actuality—never to debase man or a man to the level of a mere instrument.

Our enduring task in philosophical endeavour is to become authentic men by becoming aware of being; or, and this is the same thing: to become ourselves by achieving certainty of God. The fulfilment of this task has certain traits that remain always the same.

To-day as at all times we must do the work of the philosophical *craft*: develop the categories and methods that constitute the structure of our basic knowledge, orient ourselves in the cosmos of the sciences, assimilate the history of philosophy, practise speculative thinking in metaphysics, and apply the elucidating methods of existential philosophy.

The aim of philosophy is at all times to achieve the *independence* of man as an individual. This he gains by establishing a relation to authentic being. He gains independence of everything that happens in the world by the depth of his attachment to transcendence. What Lao-tse found in the Tao, Socrates in the divine mission and in knowledge, Jeremiah in Yahweh who revealed himself to him, what Boethius, Bruno, Spinoza knew: that was what made them independent. This philosophical independence must be confused neither with the sovereign arbitrariness of libertinism, nor with the vital energy that defies death.

At all times the task is marked by this *contradiction*: independence is to be found in aloofness from the world, in renunciation and solitude—or in the world itself, through the world, participating in the world, but without succumbing to it. Then the philosopher, who desires his freedom only with the freedom of others, his life only in communication with men, is what the fool called Confucius: 'That is the man who knows it's impossible and yet carries on'—a truth applying to the finite knowledge that absolutizes its phenomenality, but a truth that does not shake the profounder truth of philosophical faith.

Philosophy addresses itself to the individual. In every world, in every situation philosophical endeavour throws the individual back upon himself. For only he who is himself—and can prove himself in solitude—can truly enter into communication.

Now, can we, within these enduring tasks of philosophy which I have formulated, say something of its present mission?

We have heard that faith in reason is at an end. The great step taken in the twentieth century, it is said, is the falling away from the *logos*, the idea of a world order. Some exult in the consciousness that life has been liberated—others castigate this great betrayal of the mind, this catastrophe that must lead to the destruction of humanity.

On this point it can be said that the step in question implies an element of truth, because it destroyed the self-assurance of an intelligence forsaken by reason, unmasked the illusion of a world harmony, ended our reliance in the rule of law and in laws as such. These were high-sounding words behind which was hidden the sordidness of a life that was disclosed by psychoanalysis. This psychotherapeutic movement broadened into a pseudo-philosophy which took its partial truth from its relation to and dependence on a corrupt age.

When all this is sloughed off, the root lies bare. The root is the primal source from which we grew and which we had forgotten in the tangle of opinions, habits, ideological formulas.

To-day our task is to find in existence itself a new foundation for reason. That is the urgent task in the spiritual situation defined by Kierkegaard and Nietzsche, Pascal and Dostoievsky.

Its fulfilment cannot consist in the restoration of what has been. To-day it would seem to imply the following elements:

(1) We seek peace of mind by keeping ourselves constantly alert.

(2) We pass through nihilism to the assimilation of our tradition.

(3) We seek the purity of the sciences as a premise for the truth of our philosophy.

(4) Reason becomes a boundless desire for communication.

(1) *We seek peace of mind by keeping ourselves constantly alert.*

Peace of mind is the aim of philosophical thought.

Amid the greatest devastation, we should like to be certain of what remains, for that is everlasting.—In distress we reflect upon our primal source.—Amid the threat of death, we seek a thought that will make us steadfast.

Even to-day philosophy can give us what Parmenides knew when he built a shrine to the god in thanksgiving for the peace of mind that had come to him through philosophy. But to-day there is so much complacency.

It is a terrifying fact that to-day, despite all the upheaval and devastation, we are still in danger of living and thinking as though nothing really important had happened. It is as though a great misfortune had merely disturbed the good life of us poor victims, but as though life might now be continued in the old way. It is as though nothing had happened. Fearful or helpless or enraged at the moment, we accuse others. Anyone who feels in this way is still caught in snares that make possible only a delusive peace of mind. This peace must be transformed into unpeace. For the great danger is that what has happened may pass, considered as nothing but a great misfortune, without anything happening to us men as men, without our hearing the voice of transcendence, without our attaining to any insight and acting with insight. A tremendous decrease in clear awareness would then cause us to sink into a narrowed existence.

For the present situation and the future, we may take as a prototype for orientation, not for imitation, the age of the Jewish prophets. Caught between East and West, between the great empires of Babylonia and Egypt, Palestine suffered its political decline, torn and devastated, a political plaything of the great states, incorporated now in this one and now in that. Then prophets appeared with good counsels, Palestine must ally itself either with East or West, thus to obtain protection and friends, and to live happily. In opposition to these prophets of salvation arose the prophets of doom, who have retained their great name to this day. They saw the situation and rejected any position in favour of East or West. They foresaw the impending doom. But they did not see it as an accidental event brought about by superior war machines; they saw in it a profound meaning that went far beyond its particular manifestations. It is God who unrolls the world like a carpet. He causes the Assyrians to subject peoples upon peoples, and take them from their homes as one takes birds from their nests. He guides the course of events, men and states serve him as instruments, doing what they are intended to do, without suspecting that it is in accordance with God's will. The prophets who spoke thus desired to awaken their people and later all men. They had but one counsel: to obey God by leading a pure, ethical life. What is of the world is made from nothing and is nothing in itself. The meaning resides in what man does, in his obedience to God. And God's will is stated in the inviolable ten commandments. What God willed beyond them at any given moment, the prophets believed that they received from Him in revelation, and this they communicated. But it remained ambiguous. God does not speak to men directly. An enormous humility in non-knowledge is necessary. Job's questions find no answer. The high point of humility is the aged Jeremiah.

We are far from being prophets. The greatness of that age cannot be imitated. But by a comparison between the situations it might well be possible to indicate what spiritual unpeace might now be in place, and what sort of peace the soul might seek.

The last century does present an analogy to the prophets. Kierkegaard and Nietzsche, in their day seized with clairvoyance and horror at the course of mankind, are to-day still essential for our fundamental experience. Even now their goal, of making us truly awake, is not yet achieved.

But they themselves were exceptions, without being prototypes. To follow them is to go counter to their own will, and is impossible for anyone who understands them. They were at the same time victims and prophets of the epoch. Both contributed the profoundest truth, inseparably bound up with strange affirmations that remain alien to us. Kierkegaard gave us an interpretation of Christianity as a faith of the absurd, a faith of the negative decision according to which to choose no profession, to conclude no marriage, and to be only a martyr is to be an authentic Christian—an interpretation which, where adopted, means the end of Christianity. Nietzsche gave us his ideas of the will to power, the superman, and eternal recurrence, which though they have no doubt gone to some people's heads, are as unacceptable as what we might call Kierkegaard's excessive Christianity.

But most of the refutations of Kierkegaard and Nietzsche that have been written up to now, are based on misunderstanding and constitute a kind of invitation to continue sleeping. They contribute trivial commonplaces calculated to remove the thorn that was stuck in our conscience by Kierkegaard and Nietzsche. But there can be no authentic development of philosophy in the future, that does not effect a fundamental evaluation of these two great thinkers. For in the decay of their own work and the sacrifice of their own life, they have revealed to us the irreplaceable truths. So long as we continue to indulge in a false peace of mind, they remain an indispensable summons to be alert.

(2) *We pass through nihilism to an assimilation of tradition.*

If we refuse to be complacent, it means that nihilism is actual as a possibility of our own experience. We know the decay of valid norms, we know how precarious the world becomes when no faith, no collective self-consciousness commands adherence. A few men had such experience even in Nietzsche's time, some have had it since 1933, others more recently, but to-day there is scarcely a thoughtful man who has not had it. Perhaps we are now coming to the point at which we are ready to hear the message conveyed by all historical epochs of cultural breakdown, the call of their thinkers. Nihilism, as intellectual movement and as historical experience, becomes a transition to a profounder assimilation of historic tradition. From an early time, nihilism has not only been the road to the primal source —nihilism is as old as philosophy—but also the acid in which the gold of truth must be proved.

From the beginning there has been something irreplaceable in philosophy. Through all the change in human circumstances and the tasks of practical life, through all the progress of the sciences, all the development of the categories and methods of thought, it is for ever concerned with apprehending the one eternal truth under new conditions, with new methods and perhaps with greater possibilities of clarity.

It is our task to-day, amid the most extreme nihilism, to ascertain this truth once more. This presupposes that we assimilate our tradition: it is not enough that we know it externally, that we merely contemplate it; we must possess it inwardly as our very own.

To achieve this, philosophy proper must, among other things, reject the idea of progress, which is sound for the sciences and the implements of philosophy. The advocates of this idea falsely believed that what comes later must supplant what comes earlier, as inferior, as merely a step to further progress, as having only historical interest. In this conception the new as such is mistaken for the true. Through the discovery of this novelty, one feels oneself to be at the summit of

history. This was the basic attitude of many philosophers of past centuries. Over and over again they
believed that they had transcended the whole past by
means of something utterly new, and that thereby the
time had finally come to inaugurate the true philosophy.
This was the case with Descartes; in all modesty and
with the most justification Kant held this same belief;
it was held in arrogance by the so-called German ideal-
ists, Fichte, Hegel, Schelling; and then again by
Nietzsche. And tragedy was followed by Satyric drama.
The publication in 1910, in the first fascicle of *Logos*, of
Husserl's article on philosophy as an exact science, in
which, speaking as the most important, because
supremely consistent representative of his department,
he proclaimed that the definitive principles of philosophy were at last securely established, created a clear
dividing line between the partisans of progress and the
others. Despite all their respect for the rational discipline
of this phenomenology and of Neo-Kantianism, some
thinkers came out against these claims, and returned to
the traditional quest for eternal truth, which is the
essence of philosophy, considering that the new was
questionable and not worth striving for. Yet even so,
this tone of aggressive novelty survived and if I am not
mistaken is only now on the wane. The idea of progress was a form in which the experience of the primal
source was misconstrued as the historically new, because philosophy confused itself with modern science.
In addition, the desire for domination, power and prestige took possession of philosophy. Philosophy is some-

thing entirely different from what it appeared to be in such deviations: ever since man became philosophically conscious, he has realized the presence of eternity in the actual. To tear oneself away from the historical fundament in favour of something new, to make use of history as a quarry, from which to take material for arbitrary interpretations, that is a road that leads into the abyss of nihilism. We must neither subject ourselves to hypostatized manifestations of the past, nor irresponsibly remove ourselves from it in the enjoyment of contemplating what has been, but above all we must not tear ourselves away from the historical fundament. But if we have done so, nihilism will, by a painful operation, bring us back to the authentic truth.

Out of nihilism there was born a new fundamental approach which teaches us to take a different view of the history of philosophy. Three thousand years of the history of philosophy become as a single present. The diverse philosophical structures contain within themselves the one truth. Hegel was the first who strove to understand the unity of this thought, but he still looked on everything that had gone before as a preliminary stage and partial truth leading up to his own philosophy. But the essential thing is that we assimilate the philosophical attainments of every epoch by remaining in constantly renewed communication with the great achievements of the past, looking upon them not as transcended but as actual.

If we succeed in establishing a loving contact with all philosophical thought, then we know that our present form of philosophy also stems from the primal source, we know how indispensable is the universal tradition, the memory without which we would sink into the nothingness of a mere moment without past and future. In our temporal transience we know the actuality and simultaneity of essential truth, of the *philosophia perennis* which at all times effaces time.

(3) *We seek the purity of the sciences as premise for our philosophical thought.*

The premise of the technology that is revolutionizing our lives is modern science. But the effects of this science extend much farther. This science represents a profound turning point in the history of mankind, but unlike technology, it is fully known only to few men, and even fewer actively participate in it, whereas the mass of mankind goes on living in pre-scientific forms of thought and makes use of the results of science as formerly primitive peoples made use of European top hats, Albert chains and glass beads.

After the crude beginnings made by men of earlier epochs, particularly the Greeks, it has been the modern era, since the end of the Middle Ages, that first applied really unlimited inquiry, accompanied by boundless self-criticism, to everything that happens and can happen in the world.

Science proceeds methodically, it postulates universal acceptance, and in so far as this is the case, it does in fact obtain unanimous consent; it is critically aware of its methods, it systematically verifies the whole of its inventory at all times, it is never finished, but lives in a state of progress whose goal is unforeseeable. Whatever is manifested in the world, science makes into its object. It sharpens and clarifies our consciousness of the existent, and it provides the premises for the practical realization of goals that it does not prescribe, but which in turn become an object of its inquiry.

Science is a necessary precondition of philosophy. But the spiritual situation that has arisen as a result of science has presented philosophy with difficult new tasks. Former epochs were not as clearly aware of the urgency of these tasks as we are.

(1) Science must be made absolutely *pure*. For in practical operation and average thinking, it is shot through with non-scientific assertions and attitudes. Pure and strict science in its application to the whole sphere of the existent has been magnificently achieved by individual scientists, but on the whole our spiritual life is far removed from it.

(2) *Superstitious belief in science* must be exposed to the light of day. In our era of restless unbelief, men have snatched at science as a supposedly firm foundation, set their faith in so-called scientific findings, blindly subjected themselves to supposed experts, believed that the world as a whole could be put in order by scientific planning, expected science to provide life aims, which science can never offer—and expected a knowledge of being as a whole, which is beyond the scope of science.

(3) *Philosophy itself must be methodically re-clarified*. It is science in the age-old and enduring sense of metho-

dical thought, but it is not science in the pure modern sense of an inquiry into things, leading to universally valid, cogent knowledge, identical for all.

The fallacious identification of philosophy and science by Descartes, a misconception in keeping with the spirit of these last centuries, has made science into supposedly total knowledge and has ruined philosophy.

To-day the purity of philosophy must be gained along with the purity of science. The two are inseparable, but they are not the same thing; philosophy is neither a specialized science along with others, nor a crowning science resulting from the others, nor a foundation-laying science by which the others are secured.

Philosophy is bound to science and thinks in the medium of all sciences. Without the purity of scientific truth, the truth of philosophy is inaccessible.

Science has its own realm and is guided by philosophical ideas which grow up in all the sciences, though they themselves can never be scientifically justified.

The modern aspiration for consciousness of truth has become possible only on the basis of the sciences of the last century, but it has not yet been achieved. The work required for its realization is among the most urgent needs of the present historical moment.

In opposition to the disintegration of science into unrelated specialties, in opposition to the scientific superstition of the masses, in opposition to the superficiality brought upon philosophy by the confusion of science and philosophy—scientific research and philosophy must join hands to guide us on the path of authentic truth.

(4) *Reason becomes the desire for boundless communication.*

Through the secure validity of a common principle that permeated all everyday life, there was, almost until the present time, a cohesion among men which rarely permitted communication to become a special problem. People could content themselves with the saying: we can pray together, but not talk together. To-day, when we cannot even pray together, we are at length becoming fully aware that humanity implies unreserved communication among men.

Manifested being is fragmented by the multiplicity of our sources of faith, and of the historical form of our communities, each with its own special background. The only things we have identically in common are science and technology as reflected in the general categories of the understanding. These however are united only in an abstract, universal consciousness; in practice they serve both as weapons and media of communication.

Everything real in man is historical. But historicity means also multiple historicity. Hence the postulates of true communication are:

(1) to become concerned with the historically different without becoming untrue to one's own historicity—

(2) to reveal the relativity of scientific truth, while fully recognizing its just claims—

(3) to abandon the claim of faith to exclusivity because of the breach of communication it implies, yet without losing the absoluteness of one's own fundament—

(4) to take up the inevitable struggle with the historically different, but to sublimate the battle in the loving battle, in communication through the truth that develops when men act in common, not as abstract individuals—

(5) to orient ourselves toward the depths that are disclosed only with the division into manifold historicities, to one of which I belong, but which all concern me and which all together guide me to that source.

Philosophical faith is inseparable from complete openness to communication. For authentic truth arises only where faiths meet in the presence of the Comprehensive. Hence it is true that only believers can realize communication.—On the other hand, untruth grows out of the fixation of contents of faith that merely repel one another. Hence it is impossible to talk with fanatics. Philosophical faith sees deviltry in every compulsion to break off communication and in every desire to break off communication.

This philosophical faith in communication has been called utopian. Its critics argue that men are not so. They are moved by their passions, their will to power, their competing practical interests. Communication nearly always fails, and most certainly fails with the mass of men. The best solution, according to this view, is to subordinate men to conventions and laws, which serve to veil the general indiscipline and villainy, both of which exclude communication. To expect too much of men is the best way to ruin them.

In answer to this we may say:

(1) Men are not as they are; they themselves remain question and task: all total judgments concerning them say more than we can know.

(2) Communication in every form is so much a part of man as man in the very depth of his being, that it must always remain possible and one can never know how far it will go.

(3) The will to boundless communication is not a programme but the very essence of philosophical faith —and from it stem the particular purposes and methods of communication at all its levels.

(4) Boundless openness to communication is not the consequence of any knowledge, it is the decision to follow a human road. The idea of communication is not utopia, but faith. Each man is confronted with the question whether he strives toward it, whether he believes in it, not as in something other-worldly, but as in something utterly actual; whether he believes in our potentiality really to live together, to speak together, through this togetherness to find our way to the truth, and hereby finally to become authentically ourselves.

In our present distress, we understand that communication is the fundamental task before us. The elucidation of communication from its multiple sources in the modes of the Comprehensive is becoming a central theme of philosophical endeavour. But to carry communication in all its possibilities closer to realization, is the daily labour of philosophy.

Index

INDEX

Deification of man, 116,
  136–40, 141
Deism, 79
Demonic, the, 119
Demonology, 9, 98, 117,
  118–20, 125, 126–8, 136–7,
  139, 140, 141
Descartes, 21, 167, 171
Destruction, 117–18
Deutero-Isaiah, 43, 103
Devil, the, 119, 122
Dionysian rites, 80
Dogma, transformation of,
  107–8
Dostoievsky, 139, 161
Dynamism, 156

Ecclesiastes, 43, 98, 101
Egypt, 163
Elijah, 100
Enlightenment, 110, 145
Epistemology, 8
Europe, 152
Evolution, 62
Exclusivity, 88, 92, 94
Existence, 19–20, 29, 37, 39,
  40, 42, 48, 66
Existent, the, 143
Ezekiel, 100
Ezra, 101, 102

Faith, contents of, 34 ff.;
  nature of, 9 ff.; religious,
  84, 106
False, the, 142

Fate, 66
Fears, 85
Fichte, 167
Freedom, 68, 71, 75, 147
Führer, 155

Galileo, 10, 89
Genghis Khan, 156
Germany, 36
God, existence of, 34–6
God-man, 104
Goethe, 121, 122
Greeks, Greek thought, 41,
  43, 53, 80–1, 169
Guidance, 71–3

Happiness, 56
Haubach, Theodor, 36
Hegel, 36, 167, 168
Hierocracy, 103
Historicity, 42, 44
Hölderlin, 156–7
Hosea, 96
Husserl, 167

Ideal[s], 69, 70
Idols, 125
Immanence, 116, 118, 143
Immortality, 20
Imperative, 36–7
India, 110
Indian religion, 41, 83
Infinity, 65
Intuition, 116
Isaiah, 80, 100

178

INDEX

INDEX

DATE DUE

	261-2500		Printed in USA